Ecstatic Transformation

Ecstatic Transformation

Transpersonal Psychology
in the Work of Mechthild of Magdeburg

Ulrike Wiethaus

Syracuse University Press

Copyright © 1996 by Syracuse University Press
Syracuse, New York 13244-5160

ALL RIGHTS RESERVED

First Edition 1996

96 97 98 99 00   6 5 4 3 2 1

The paper used in this publication meets the minimum requirements of American National Standard for Information Sciences—Permanence of Paper for Printed Library Materials, ANSI Z39.48-1984. ∞™

Library of Congress Cataloging-in-Publication Data

Wiethaus, Ulrike.
    Ecstatic transformation : transpersonal psychology in the work of Mechthild of Magdeburg / Ulrike Wiethaus. — 1st ed.
        p.   cm.
    Includes bibliographical references and index.
    ISBN 0-8156-2680-0 (cloth : alk. paper). — ISBN 0-8156-0369-X (pbk. : alk. paper)
    1. Visions.   2. Mechthild, of Magdeburg, ca. 1212–ca. 1282.
3. Altered state of consciousness.   4. Transpersonal psychology.
5. Mysticism—History—Middle Ages, 600–1500.   I. Title.
BV5091.V6W54   1995
154.4—dc20   95-2911

Manufactured in the United States of America

Contents

Ulrike Wiethaus teaches in the humanities at Wake Forest University. She is the editor of *Maps of Flesh and Light: The Religious Experience of Medieval Women Mystics* (published by Syracuse University Press) and coeditor (with Karen Cherewatuk) of *Dear Sister: Medieval Women and the Epistolary Genre*. She has published numerous articles on medieval women mystics and feminist spirituality.

Ecstatic Transformation

1

Introduction

The Historical Context

$\mathcal{T}$his book attempts to answer questions about the nature of religious experiences that occur during mystical states of consciousness. It is an interdisciplinary study of contemporary theories on altered states of consciousness and the ecstasies and visions in the mystical work *Das fliessende Licht der Gottheit* (*The Flowing Light of the Godhead*) by the thirteenth-century Beguine Mechthild of Magdeburg (ca. 1208–1282).[1]

Because of its interdisciplinary approach, the book can be read for two reasons. One is simply to learn more about some aspects of the extraordinary mysticism of Mechthild of Magdeburg, whose literary, theological, and spiritual sophistication deserves more recognition in the United States than it has as yet received. Another reason to open the book, however, is to engage in a dialogue between religion and humanistic and transpersonal psychologies. Given the growing interest in spirituality and the birth of new paradigms that merge insights from Jewish, Christian, Buddhist, humanistic, neopagan, and nu-

1. All translations of texts from *The Flowing Light of the Godhead* are mine. For a full English translation, I refer the reader to Mechthild von Magdeburg's *Flowing Light of the Divinity* trans. Christiane Mesch Galvani (1991). I have based my translations on the editions of Mechthild of Magdeburg by P. Gall Morell (1980) and Hans Neumann (1991). The parenthetical citations refer to the books and chapters of *The Flowing Light of the Godhead*.

merous other traditions, it is important to reflect upon the contributions of analytical frameworks. This book is divided into two parts. Part 1 presents a discussion of ecstasies. Chapters 1 and 2 describe Mechthild's historical and cultural context, the questions that this context raises for us today methodologically (especially from a women's studies point of view), and the characteristics of ecstatic experiences in *The Flowing Light of the Godhead*. Chapters 3 and 4 focus on contemporary psychological theories of ecstasy and contrast them with Mechthild's teachings. The second part of the book offers an analysis of some of Mechthild's visions (chapter 5) and compares them with contemporary psychophysiological approaches to visionary phenomena.

My approach to Mechthild's work is governed by the question of how Western mysticism can be made intellectually accessible to a contemporary audience. I chose humanistic and transpersonal psychologies as a framework in my search for an answer. Researchers and therapists who have produced significant work in this area are biased positively toward religious experience and often claim mystics as their predecessors.

The key term that guides my use of humanistic psychologies is *self-actualization*, a concept that has been introduced to a larger audience in the United States by Abraham Maslow. In regard to transpersonal psychologies, I am primarily interested in their description and definition of *altered states of consciousness*. I use these two terms as approximate twentieth-century equivalents of the medieval mystical concepts of *deificatio* (to abolish identification with one's human nature and recognize one's own divine core), *visio* (vision) and *alienatio mentis/ fruitio/raptus* (ecstasy). Medieval theologians developed sophisticated typologies of ecstatic and visionary experiences; most of these models were second-order discussions or "language games," that is, reflections upon rather than expressions of mystical experiences. Within the framework of my study, these taxonomies are subordinated to Mechthild's own set of distinctions.[2]

The theory of self-actualization, like its approximate medieval precursor *deificatio*, is based on the assumption that every human being has the potential to become something qualitatively better and should strive to manifest this potential. Both the medieval and the contemporary models operate on the assumption that a "higher" spiritual realm exists that is accessible to human consciousness through spontaneous or intentional action. The terms "self-actualization" and *deificatio* are somewhat misleading as to their point of reference. To truly become *one/self*, according to Maslow, is a paradox, since the actualizing self expands its boundaries through a growing awareness and appreciation of the concerns, needs, and sheer existence of others (Maslow 1971). Similarly, *deificatio* in most medieval mystical theories is not about becoming godlike in an absolutist, transtemporal and transmaterial sense, but means the unfolding of one's full prelapsarian humanness. The process of *deificatio* thus has a redemptive quality. At least in the late Middle Ages, it centers on the imitation of the human manifestation of the divine, Christ *(imitatio Christi)*. The theoretical concepts of self-actualization and *deificatio* overlap in their emphasis on the importance of ethical values and involvement with others, a dimension that is often missing in transpersonal analyses of religious phenomena.[3]

The understanding of visions and ecstasies varied widely during the medieval period. By the late Middle

2. For studies on medieval mystical taxonomies, see Clark 1992; McGinn 1991; Hummel 1989; Idel 1988; Wrede 1974; and Pike 1992.

3. See Sheldrake 1992 for an excellent discussion of the relationship between medieval spirituality, including the Beguines, and contemporary spirituality.

Ages (ca. 1200–1500), the Western mystical tradition began to be shaped by an astonishingly large number of religious women; male mystics and visionaries from this period are rare. The women often created the first religious texts in their native languages, because either they or their audiences could not speak or write Latin. Their form of mysticism is generally defined as experiential or practical, since its core is determined by physiospiritual encounters with Christ as lover, *Minnechristus* (*Minne* is the Middle High German term for courtly love), and as sufferer, *Passionschristus*, rather than theological abstraction (Bynum 1989; Dinzelbacher, 1989a, 89; Lochrie 1991; Beer 1992; Clark 1992; Petroff 1994). Thus Mechthild of Magdeburg was part of a larger Western European movement, which endorsed women as spiritual teachers, prophets, and models of piety. Whereas ecstasies tended to be intense states of emotional intimacy with Christ, medieval visions were shamanic journeys into supernatural realms (heaven, purgatory, or hell), from which the mystic returned with messages that were crucial for the well-being of a community (Le Goff, 1984; Dinzelbacher, 1989a; Gardiner, 1989; Czerwinski, 1993). Many of the visions of Birgitta of Sweden (ca. 1302–1373) or Catherine of Siena (1347–1380), for example, were aimed at the ecclesiastical elites; the visions of Mechthild of Magdeburg or Hadewijch (first half of thirteenth century), on the other hand, appear to have been intended for a relatively select group of spiritually minded lay and religious people of both sexes.

When we compare the attitude toward altered states of consciousness in transpersonal psychology and medieval people's attitude toward visions that were accepted as divinely inspired (devils and demons had the power to induce visions as well), a number of striking differences emerge.

Peter Dinzelbacher (1989a, 5–6) points out that:

1. Visions appear to have occurred more frequently during the Middle Ages than today; among other things, this phenomenon led to the creation of a distinct literary genre, the *Offenbarungsliteratur* (revelation literature).

2. Unlike in religious systems of some non-Western cultures and during the sixties in the United States and in Western Europe, visions were not induced by drugs (for an alternative view, see Ginzburg 1985, 1991). Personal and communal preparations for visions included prayer, meditation, and ascetic exercises, although orthodox visions were consistently interpreted as gifts of divine grace.

3. The content of visions was congruent with widespread cultural themes that found expression in medieval art, sculpture, and literature. Within a Christian framework, the imaginistic continuity between the twelfth and twentieth century, with its focus on a human Christ and the Virgin Mary, has been greater than that between the early and late Middle Ages.

4. Medieval visions tended to result in concrete changes of behavior on the part of the visionary or her audience, usually in the form of religious and socially relevant activities, such as the founding of a monastery or hospital, the writing of a book, or a more pious lifestyle (see also Kleinberg 1991). Experiences of altered states of consciousness in transpersonal literature are far less socially oriented and focus instead on personal insight and spiritual knowledge.

5. Medieval visionaries and their audiences assumed the existence of a spiritual realm beyond the human psyche; contemporary "maps" chart transpersonal realms as inner-psychic worlds of "consciousness." Although this consciousness is often postulated as existing independently from the neurological structures of the brain (see Grof 1985), symbols and images that occur during

visionary experiences are interpreted cautiously as metaphorical rather than literal in contemporary society.

In summary, visionary experiences were more relevant to medieval people's daily lives and were applied in numerous ways for socially relevant purposes. This is certainly not the case for contemporary Western society, where altered states of consciousness play at best a marginal role.

In his useful overview, Dinzelbacher unfortunately omitted the important factor of gender in comparing medieval and contemporary uses of visions. As noted above, the visionaries of the High Middle Ages were almost exclusively female. This circumstance raises some feminist questions. Did the visionary mode augment or diminish the social status of religious women? Did it support or impede women's development of basic skills and special talents (see Finke 1993)? Did it engender a distinctly feminine religious tradition? Could the women mystics have helped create a cultural climate favorable to women? In view of contemporary feminist spirituality, can women claim mystics such as Mechthild of Magdeburg as foremothers and models? The first question cannot be answered in the positive, because women mystics received their status not through their visions as such, but via authorization by an all-male ecclesiastical hierarchy. However, the increase in number of women visionaries coincided with the growth of the universities, to which women were barred admission. Having only secondhand access to theological knowledge, women often used visions as an alternative mode of "doing theology" and as a means of participating actively in religious discourse. Finding a means of participation was all the more vital for medieval women's sense of self-determination if we keep in mind that religion was then far more significant as a *weltanschauung* than today. That the visionary mode benefited the cultivation of a woman's talents is quite obvious: they incited women to write, to think, to compose, to counsel, to become publicly active, to travel, to overcome timidity and self-doubt. From a feminist perspective, the historian Gerda Lerner has argued that medieval mysticism afforded women opportunities to forge pockets of resistance and provided modes of authentic self-expression even in a patriarchal society (Lerner 1993).

In terms of developing a sense of self, I suggest that ecstasies and visions were often used as a medium to explore and define self and world in marked juxtaposition to existing and newly emerging misogynist views (see also Poor 1994). A flexible enough symbolic superstructure allowed for a Christian interpretation of women's experiences that supported their experiments, in particular in the figures of a loving and accepting Virgin Mary and Christ. A stern and judgmental father figure is often tellingly absent in their symbolic universe.

If we read the texts by medieval women mystics not only as somewhat stereotyped reflections of their times (which they were to a certain extent), but also as experimental explorations, we find that they parallel in a perhaps surprising way contemporary women's spiritual journeys. Both contemporary and medieval women engage(d) in the development and refinement of marginalized symbol systems within the Western tradition that allow for the expression of women's concerns, questions, and desires. Also, the late Middle Ages and the twentieth century have a common denominator, although manifested in different forms: patriarchal social structures and ideologies. Whereas medieval women mystics cannot be described as separatist as the women today who claim a "WomanChurch" in temporary exile (Ruether 1988), both groups use(d) of the medium of altered states of consciousness as a heuristic alternative to male-dominated discourse.

Contemporary Definitions of Consciousness

Ecstasies today are often not claimed in some supernatural realm, but in the physical world. Feminist spirituality celebrates and values *Eros* as physiospiritual ecstatic
dimension and path—from the poetic *The Three Marias* by
the Portuguese writers Maria Isabel Barreno, Maria Teresa Horta, and Maria Velho da Costa (1973) to Carter
Heyward's theological work *Touching our Strength: The
Erotic as Power and the Love of God* (1989). Visions in the
form of dreams, poetic inspirations, and artistic creativity
are accepted sources for building new theologies and
spiritualities (see, for example, Christ 1980; Morton 1985;
Allen 1986; Eller, 1993). Furthermore, women's self-actualization today has often been described as a change of
consciousness. Here, the term *consciousness* is used to denote distinct sets of values and motivations. Women
need to understand their oppression within a patriarchal
system that creates and perpetuates a consciousness of
victimization. Only then can liberating images of oneself
and others, which are rooted in values such as mutuality,
form an affirmation of uniqueness and diversity, and
courage rather than opportunism.

Female alienation, the "state of consciousness" that
often forms the ground and beginning of spiritual self-
exploration, has been described succinctly by Janice Raymond (1987). She isolates three fundamental attitudes.
Dissociation is the refusal to take part in a "man-made"
society. The characteristics of this attitude are passivity,
powerlessness, and a "worm's eye view of the world"
(167). *Assimilation* refers to co-opting oneself. Stereotypes
of femininity are internalized to the extent that expressions of authenticity and spontaneity are stifled. In comparison to a state of dissociation, this attitude provides a
larger measure of success and influence in an androcentric setting; one plays by the rules and is rewarded for

it. *Victimism*, finally, negates "Self-definition and Self-re-sponsibility in the world. When women do not define themselves beyond the role of the sufferer, then women will settle for the world as men have made it. Victimism means being overwhelmed by the world" (172). Although Raymond does not address the topic explicitly, these psychological responses to patriarchy have also informed women's religious behavior. Victimism and assimilation have often been synonymous for women in Christianity, with its feminine ideal of silent endurance and patient suffering. Dissociation is the most oppositional of the three attitudes and because of its voicelessness the most difficult to document.

How can we connect the definition of woman's consciousness implicit in Raymond, which revolves around the dialectic of oppression and liberation, with that of humanistic and transpersonal psychology? It is helpful to begin with definitions of consciousness and awareness given by *Webster's New International Dictionary*, 3d ed. The term *consciousness* refers on the one hand to the "totality of sensations, perceptions, ideas, attitudes, and feelings." The insight that this totality, contained and ordered as consciousness, is also dependent upon psychological, social, and political circumstance was the focus of political analyses that preceded feminist political thought (for example, Fanon 1967). Anthropologists provided another clue in their descriptions of the relation between altered states of consciousness (such as trance and spirit possession) and consciousness as a set of values and motivations (see Taussig 1987). Numerous studies demonstrated how disenfranchised members of revitalization movements such as cargo cults used altered states as a coping response to extreme experiences of political and economical oppression and deprivation. Through shifting awareness, cult members could release feelings of helplessness and frustration. The experiential contact with divine forces enabled them to confront and transcend destructive internalized value patterns and regain a sense of self-determination and self-respect. Anthony Wallace called this complex process a "mazeway reformulation" (Wallace 1956).

The psychospiritual technique of revitalization movements is somewhat similar to the work of feminists interested in spirituality. It is acknowledged that the consciously manufactured shift from principal states (normal waking states) to alternate states of consciousness such as mild trances, relaxed receptive moods, or excited affective states allows an influx of imagery and ideas that can serve as a corrective and alternative to dominant paradigms experienced as stifling and oppressive. To this purpose, spiritual feminists employ a wide spectrum of techniques that include rituals, meditation, self-hypnosis, chanting, dancing, relaxation techniques, visualizations, and more (Eller 1993). In this case, consciousness defined as content is complemented by a definition of consciousness as *awareness*.

Webster's describes consciousness also as "awareness or perception of an inward psychological or spiritual fact: intuitively perceived knowledge of something in one's inner self." Spiritually minded feminists mythologize this use of altered states by pronouncing that intuition has been a specifically female domain for thousands of years (see, for example, Mariechild 1981; Muehlmann 1981; Starhawk 1982; Perrone, Stockel, and Krueger 1989). Within the context of this study, the point can be made that white Western women do not have to retrieve their traditions from a mythological past that is difficult to reconstruct. The testimonies by and about European medieval women mystics provide ample material to recover a more tangible, better documented, and consequently more challenging tradition.

The creative use of altered states for a project of

"mazeway resynthesis" calls into question our culture's extreme bias toward "normal" or "principal" states of consciousness. Might such bias not waste mental resources that have significant adaptive potential? Apart from their accepted employment in nonwhite, non-Western cultures, relaxation and visualization exercises are not just used by "new age" feminists, but are becoming acceptable means in mainstream psychotherapy. Psychoanalysis has utilised dreams and the dynamics of free association during a state of relaxation from its very beginnings (see Kakar 1991).

A more positive definition of states of consciousness that eliminates the value-laden designations "principal," "ordinary," and "altered" has been proposed by the psychiatrist and transpersonal psychologist Stanislav Grof. He distinguishes between *hylotropic* and *holotropic* consciousness (Grof 1985). *Hylotropic* consciousness

> involves the experience of oneself as a solid physical entity with definite boundaries and a limited sensory range, living in three-dimensional space and linear time in the world of material objects. Experiences in this mode systematically support a number of basic assumptions, such as: matter is solid; two objects cannot simultaneously occupy the same space; past events are irretrievably lost; future events are not experientially accessible; one cannot be in more than one place at a time; one can exist only in a single framework at a time . . . (Grof 1985, 345)

Grof defines *holotropic* awareness as independent from the coordinates of space and time and the laws of matter as defined in a Newtonian universe. It

> involves identification with a field of consciousness with no definite boundaries which has unlimited experiential access to different aspects of reality without the

mediation of the senses. A subject may experience numerous alternatives to three-dimensional space and linear time. . . . Time and space are ultimately arbitrary;
the same space can be simultaneously occupied by
many objects; the past and the future can be brought
experientially into the present moment . . . (Grof 1985,
346; see also Lightman 1993)

Hylotropic and holotropic consciousness could coexist
side by side in Western medieval society, which has often
been characterized as the "age of belief" or as "archaic"
(Ginzburg 1985, 1992; Czerwinski 1993). Having been edited out from the spectrum of consciousness in our society, the use of holotropic awareness is now confined to
carefully circumscribed social groups (for example, ar-
tists) and selective situations (for example, getting drunk
at socially acceptable occasions, nighttime dreaming, or
during episodes of "mental illness" in otherwise healthy
individuals). Social control and a general mistrust of holotropic consciousness become particularly evident when
it is used as an act of social defiance or cultural resistance. The exploration of hallucinogens during the sixties
or the 1990 Supreme Court decision against the use of
peyote in Native American religions are two recent examples. From this perspective, *self-actualization* and *states of
consciousness*, the two terms with which I began my discussion, are indeed interrelated. Experiencing and ex-
ploring the different worlds of hylotropic and holotropic
consciousness in a sustained fashion relativizes the dominance of either state. It "deautomatizes" (a term coined
by Arthur Deikman, 1982) the use of fixed cognitive systems and challenges their monopoly on our understanding of "reality." It thus increases our capacity as a culture
to develop human creative potential and possibilities for
positive social change. Furthermore, this process allows
hitherto unconscious material to emerge and be used

constructively in times of individual or collective crises (see Turner 1977).

As experts on altered states have pointed out, however, the exploration of a holotropic state can be dangerous if stable and supportive superstructures are missing. Medieval mystics were embedded in a closely knit community of women and men who observed their every step, provided them with a collectively accepted interpretative system, and prevented them from self-inflicted harm during ecstatic states. Students of the Kabbala, to cite an example from another religious tradition, lived in close contact with their masters and were barred from studying kabbalistic texts until they reached full adulthood and had absorbed vast theological materials (Idel 1988).

Based on his work with clients, Grof noted the following about the benefits and potential difficulties (in Western society) regarding holotropic states:

> A life experience focusing exclusively on the hylotropic mode and systematically denying the holotropic one is ultimately unfulfilling and fraught with lack of meaning, but can be practiced without any major emotional difficulties. A selective and exclusive focus on the holotropic mode is incompatible with adequate functioning in the material world for the time it lasts. Like the hylotropic mode, it can be difficult or pleasant, but it presents no major problems as long as the external situation of the experiencer is covered. Psychopathological problems result from a clash and disharmonic mixture of the two modes when neither of them is experienced in pure form nor integrated with the other into an experience of a higher order. (Grof 1985, 347)

As Grof points out correctly at the end of this quotation, it is not enough simply to experience different states of consciousness. Experiences need to be integrated, their contents reflected upon and compared to already existing spiritual traditions. The quality of a resulting spirituality is often dependent upon the capacity of the subject to work intensively with her material. The remarkable theological legacy of Julian of Norwich (ca. 1343–after 1416), for example, is based on a series of visions that she received on a single day. The fact that the subject's theological training is implemental in the understanding and use of new data explains, at least to a certain degree, the wide range of mystical literature and its mixtures of diverse cultural motifs. Previous knowledge can both highlight and restrict what is seen or heard in the holotropic mode. Ignatius of Loyola (1491–1556), for example, described an incident in which he learned to appropriate an unrecognizable visionary object through available religious categories. He was repeatedly puzzled by an ambiguous apparition that he could not decipher for many years. An aesthetically pleasing undulating form with what resembled many eyes, it seemed alive but was unintelligible to him until he finally saw it juxtaposed with a Christian icon, the cross. Against the background of the cross, the shimmering image coagulated into that of a snake, which he was then able to interpret as a manifestation of the devil (Ignatius of Loyola *Autobiography*, 1986, 256, 261; see also Meissner 1992, pt. 5).

A more recent example can be found in the classic study of holotropic states by Richard M. Bucke (1837–1902), for which he coined the term *cosmic consciousness* (Bucke 1961). *Cosmic consciousness* denotes a state that is exclusively noetic; in the flash of a second, subjects feel flooded with spiritual knowledge. It includes the realization that the universe is a living, vibrating whole, that all beings are connected for the good of all, and that there is life after death (Bucke 1961, 63). Bucke's culture and his own intellectual choice of a frame of reference, however,

did not prepare him to integrate the content of his illumination fully into hylotropic states. Therefore, his discussion of this state is filled with racial and sexist
stereotypes, which allow him to assign cosmic consciousness as an "evolutionary achievement" to the "superior
race" of "Aryan peoples" (45–49), and in that race to the
privileged minds of "individuals mostly of the male sex,
who are otherwise highly developed—men of good intellect, of high moral qualities, of superior physique" (55).

This hierarchical and oppressive framework is in stark
contrast to the content of a state of cosmic consciousness,
which stresses the unity and interdependency of all life
forms. Would Bucke have chosen to translate the message of his mystical experiences into his methodology,
he would have found an overwhelming mass of evidence
of cosmic consciousness among women, whether European (women mystics such as Mechthild of Magdeburg)
or African-American (for example, Rebecca Jackson or
Jarena Lee), and members of preindustrial non-Western
cultures.

In sum, state-dependent self-actualization is intri-
cately linked with motivation, which in turn is dependent
upon what ideals of self and community a particular society propagates for its members and how far a subject is
willing or able to deviate from those ideals. In order for
holotropic consciousness to be effective socially, a stable
social infrastructure needs to exist so that the knowledge
gained in altered states can be shared, disseminated, and
reflected upon.

Women and Religious Experience in
Thirteenth-century Europe

In terms of theological achievements, the thirteenth
century has been lauded as the climax of medieval cul-

ture, as "one of the 'classical' ages [in the history of Western culture], when human civilization, that slow, thorny cactus, suddenly flowers, and . . . compensates the historian for the barren prospect of a thousand years of stupidity and barbarism" (Fremantle 1984, 72). In view of the theological, spiritual, and ecclesiastical accomplishments of the twelfth century, this judgment aims perhaps a bit too high (see, for example, Southern 1970; Chenu 1968; McGinn 1987). One remarkable characteristic of the thirteenth century, however, certainly supports at least those scholars who define human civilization on the basis of the cultural and economic influence of women: the astounding rise and creativity of women mystics throughout Western Europe (Southern 1970; Dinzelbacher and Bauer 1985; Petroff 1986; Bynum 1987). Among the early centers of this movement were the Netherlands and Belgium, where religious women lived as Beguines or were affiliated with Cistercian houses. In the first half of the thirteenth century, women mystics figured predominantly in the northeastern part of Germany. Helfta in Saxony was the home of Gertrud the Great (1256–1301/02), Mechthild of Hackeborn (1241/42–1299), and Mechthild of Magdeburg in her old age (Bynum 1982, 170–263; Finnegan 1991). Elisabeth of Thuringia (1207–1231) and Jutta of Sangershausen (1220–1260) are also among the better known religious women from this part of Germany. From the second half of the thirteenth century onwards, German-speaking women mystics flourished in the west and southwest regions. The female Dominican monasteries of Unterlinden, Katharinenthal, Engelthal, and Töss, to name just a few, produced an enormous wealth of women's spiritual biographies (Ringler 1980). A third significant center evolved in the north of Italy, where women attached themselves to the mendicant orders. Examples of outstanding mystics of this region are Claire of Assisi (1193/4–1253), Angela of Foligno

(1248–1309), and Margaretha of Cortona (1247–1297) (see Petroff 1994).

Within the context of German mysticism, Mechthild's writings have been praised as the oldest qualitatively outstanding text in the German vernacular, a work of unusual vitality that reaches far beyond ordinary spiritual perception. In its poetry it embodies to some interpreters the "primal sound of divine eros" (Schmidt 1985, 123). These tributes to Mechthild are by no means understatements. Her texts entice the reader with their aesthetic beauty, the power and freshness of their imagery, and the subtlety of their theological thought. Mechthild lived and explored a cosmos that breathes passion and love. What is today reduced to a phenomenon peculiar to the human psyche revealed itself to Mechthild as a cosmic, transpersonal pattern. Mechthild's theology of this divine force as intimate, personalistic, and dialogical anticipates Martin Buber's concept of the "I-Thou" relationship and blends it at times with the awesomeness of Rudolf Otto's vision of the *tremendum fascinosum*, the holy as simultaneously fear-inspiring *and* deeply attractive.

The mysticism of *The Flowing Light of the Godhead* is part of the *Brautmystik* or nuptial mysticism that originated with Bernard of Clairvaux (1090–1153) in his commentaries on the Song of Songs (Matter 1990, 123–51). The symbolism of the *Brautmystik* allocates to the human Christ the role of the bridegroom and to the human soul the role of beloved bride. As E. Ann Matter points out, the Cistercian interpretation of this symbolism stressed the weakness and imperfection of the soul "which leads to the necessity for spiritual ascent, the ultimate goal of the monastic life. In this, the Cistercians seem particularly aware of the limitations of not just the body, but even the soul in this world, and look ahead, with trembling love and fear, to a hoped-for mystical consummation of the world to come" (1990, 133). Mechthild of

Magdeburg and other women mystics such as Hadewijch pulled this otherworldly theological thrust back into the orbit of a less dualistic, soul-affirming human universe. Intense union, no matter how short-lived, is possible even while living in this body on earth, they claim. The reason: despite the fall, God still acknowledges and desires the soul in her full likeness to her divine Thou. To quote Mechthild: "And our savior became bridegroom. . . . The bride became drunk seeing the noble countenance. . . . Our savior became bridegroom in the joyful ecstasy of the trinity. When God could not remain within himself, he created the soul and gave himself to her in great love" (1, 22).

In its spiritual core, human existence is not governed by fear and trembling, but by self-confidence and self-assertion that is sustained by the knowledge of being loved. "I am born noble and free" (2, 19), the soul proclaims. Surely, Bernard of Clairvaux's theological discussion of human freedom reverberates in these words, in particular his notion of freedom from sorrow (see McGinn 1987, 324–26). Combined with her ecstatic insistence upon the equality of bride and bridegroom, however, Mechthild's poetic description of human freedom and dignity evoke an existential depth level of harmony not to be found in Bernard. In a sense, Mechthild anticipates the cosmic optimism for which Julian of Norwich became known. Unlike Julian's calm assurance that "all will be well, and every kind of thing will be well," however, Mechthild's ecstatic vision of harmony between divinity and humanity is sensual, erotic and exuberant.

Thus her writings were not mere speculation, but accounts of actual experiences that posited body and soul in an intense (yet not unproblematic) relationship to each other. For Mechthild, as for many other medieval mystics—particularly women—the sacred knew how to speak the language of the body, even if it was not of the body, and transgressed not just linguistically, but often also experientially the boundary between immaterial and material dimensions.[4]

It is possible to interpret the particular emotional nature of *The Flowing Light of the Godhead* and similar texts as a response to cultural and economic changes in late medieval society. The assumptions about the nature of sacred reality implicit in visionary accounts were drawn from a socioreligious *weltanschauung* that had undergone great conceptual transformations in the preceding two centuries. Peter Brown has argued that around the year 1000 C.E., the realms of the sacred and the profane were still merged without noticeable divisions (Peter Brown 1975). This conceptual fusion paralleled a social structure that was based more on consensus than on authority. Until approximately the twelfth century, the body politic consisted of family groupings of relatively equal social status, whose relationships were finely balanced. This balance was achieved and maintained by a rigid set of values. According to Brown, the sacred functioned within this system as "the depository of the objectified values of the group. . . . the sacred, therefore, was intimately connected with the life of the group on every level. At the same time, however, it was operative because it was thought of as radically different from the human world into which it penetrated. It was all the community was

4. It is still a matter of debate whether medieval mystics as a group denied or affirmed the body. To pose the question indicates a twentieth-century concern; the common denominator for all discussions is certainly that medieval women mystics used the body as a metaphor for communicating and experiencing their spirituality, whether "positively" or "negatively." For a position that interprets the women mystics' bodily consciousness as affirmative, see Bynum 1989. For a position that argues for a sublimated and transformed sensuality, see Schmidt 1986. My own stand in regard to the special case of three female representatives of bridal mysticism is spelled out in Wiethaus 1991.

not" (1975, 140, 141). Mircea Eliade has argued that this attitude toward the sacred is characteristic of primal or indigenous cultures: the sacred represents reality, and anything—time, space, creatures—becomes real only insofar as it can participate in the sacred (Eliade 1959b; see also Czerwinski 1993).

This finely tuned model lost its relevance when northern European society became more diverse, flexible, and expansive. Previously rigid social structures broke down and entered a state of flux. Instead of decisions made predominantly by consensus, authority of one group over another began to govern social contracts. In literature, the arts, and religion, a very gradual process began in which the subjective and individual dimension of experience supplemented and eventually partially replaced the objective and collective (Bynum 1982; Aers 1988). As a result, the conceptualization of the holy changed as well to include individualized feelings and needs. Hence (at least in part) the renewed emphasis on Christ's humanity in the twelfth century and the emergence of a spirituality and a mystical tradition that stressed affect. In his survey of visionary literature, for example, Dinzelbacher sees the twelfth century as an "axial period" in which visions about the afterlife become replaced by visions of personal encounters with Christ. The former describe elaborate "funerary geographies" (Eliade's term) replete with geographical details and populated with a great many actors, whereas the latter tend to exclude spatial references in preference to intimate scenarios of the heart (Dinzelbacher 1989a, 21). According to Brown, the supernatural turned into "an upward extension of the individual. The supernatural becomes an awareness of the individual's own potentiality, salvaged by being raised above the ambiguities and illusions of the natural world" (1975, 146).

Although Mechthild wrote for both men and women,

the potentiality that Brown points to differed in meaning for each gender group in terms of access to religious authority. The inherent contradictions between the (male) ecclesiastical, hierarchical mode and the (female) mystical, experiential mode came to reflect the problematic relationship between men and women in church and society and necessarily created conflicts of authority and religiously articulated identity (for Mechthild's conflicts with authority, see Poor 1994). A more intimate and personalized understanding of the divine posed the danger of undermining the church's claims to hegemonic authority, even if that was not the mystics' intention. It is not by accident that Mechthild was attacked because of an account of a eucharistic vision in which the mass was celebrated without a priest. Recently, eucharistic visions of female mystics in particular have been interpreted as compensations for their lack of social power (Bynum 1987; Petroff 1994; see also Rubin 1992). As such, they represent an example of "mazeway resynthesis" and resistance to oppressive social dynamics. Although the visionary mode did not aid women in securing long-term institutionalized access to significant positions of power, it allowed them at least for a time to influence and shape already existing symbol systems rather than just emulating them. In this, they profited from the larger sociocultural paradigm shift from a collective to an individualized vision of reality.[5]

The following chapter presents a discussion of the ways in which Mechthild of Magdeburg took advantage of the creative freedom that such an increase in individualization offered. Ecstasies, intense psychophysiological experiences of the divine, allowed Mechthild to reflect on traditional spiritual teachings and to reformulate them for her community.

5. See Kagan 1990 for a fascinating Counter-Reformation example.

2

Ecstatic Experiences in
The Flowing Light of the Godhead

*I*n the following analysis of Mechthild's ecstasies and visions, I will focus in particular on Books 1 and 2, because
they offer her teachings on altered states in a remarkably
compact form (a summary of Mechthild's ecstatic teachings in Books 2 to 7 can be found in pages 38–57).
Accounts of her ecstasies in the first book are contained
in forty-six chapters of varying length. The relative short-
ness of the chapters and the organic rather than systematic order in which they are presented offer a clue to the
function of the text within a community of readers. Because each section can stand by itself, it appears that they
have all been written as short contemplative pieces to be
read, discussed, and meditated upon during gatherings.
As such, they form a sort of public, communally shared
florilegium. The text comprises poems, various forms of
dialogue, aphorisms, prayers, short pieces of prose, and
sequences that seem to function as commentaries on
theological topics.[1] Some of the chapters appear to be

---

1. Heinz Tillmann distinguished between developed and undeveloped dialogue forms. The undeveloped dialogue comprises the address in prayer and hymnic form, the "semi-dialogue" in indirect
speech and the simple question-answer scheme. A developed dialogue consists of an exchange of statements varying from four or five
up to twenty to twenty-five units. Tillmann found that 58 percent of
the dialogues are spoken by God and the soul, 63 percent are pure

written consecutively and deal with a common theme; others seem to be loosely connected and cover a variety of spiritual issues. The diversity of the texts, which might appear confusing at first glance, can be fully appreciated only if we see them within a larger context of oral discourse; as in a parish community today, for example, issues and topics in Mechthild's spiritual community varied from week to week based on the liturgical calendar, yet they must also have been related to the day-to-day questions and concerns of its members.

A number of scholars have suggested that Mechthild intended her works as diary or autobiography, an interpretation reflecting the fact that many of her writings are related to her personal experiences.[2] In the prologue, Mechthild writes explicitly that the book talks only about herself and her secret. Perceptible changes in her style and topics as she gets older also provide clues to her inner development. Nonetheless, many examples make the definition of her text as diary or autobiography unlikely: the frequent remarks to an audience, the hortatory style of some chapters (e.g., 1, 7; 1, 10; 1, 27), the intentional translation of personal experience into a model that can be followed by all "spiritual people," and numorous impersonal reflections on topics of general religious interest.

The Flowing Light of the Godhead uses clearly distinguishable poetic forms, but it does not conform unequiv-

---

dialogue, 38 percent are invocations, and in the work as a whole 34 percent of the formal structure represents a dialogue in one form or another (1933, 14–15). For a discussion of Mechthild's use of different genres, see Poor 1994).

2. See Ruth Anne Dick Abraham, "Mechthild of Magdeburg's *Flowing Light of the Godhead:* An Autobiographical Realization of Spritual Poverty" (Ph.D. diss., Stanford University, 1980), 27. She suggested that "the *Flowing Light* is an autobiography which describes a particular person only to transcend the particularity of this person in fiction." On the diary form of the text see also Tillmann 1933, 1–4 and Zinter 1931, 7.

ocally to any "classic" medieval rhyme or dialogue scheme as used by the *Minnesang* tradition or in folk songs.[3] Some texts are reminiscent of liturgical passages, but as in the case of other literary forms, the author soon abandons structural laws in favor of a personalized style. Freedom from commonly used literary patterns is also mentioned in the discussion of works of such women writers as Christine de Pisan, the women troubadours of the Langue d'Oc, and Marie de France (Wilson 1984). Hildegard of Bingen's *music* is praised with a similar judgment (Kazarow 1993).[4] It has been suggested that this is a commonly shared feature among medieval female authors. Their creative freedom, expressed in greater personal involvement of the author and less conventional development of plot and characters, may be related to women's marginal status in medieval society: they had no need to yield to the pressures of competition male writers faced in gaining social recognition and subsistence.[5] In Mechthild's case, the lack of scholastic theological training and her double marginality as Beguine and woman may in part account for her originality. Literary critics less concerned with the sociological background of Mechthild's creativity stress her poetic talent, an "immense liveliness" and a "powerful urge" to articulate her feelings and visions (Zinter 1931, 5), and his highly developed "creative power" (Tillmann 1933, 85).

3. Tillmann (1933, 4) listed epic forms, lyrics, and didactic sections. In terms of style, he emphasized Mechthild's prose and lyrical passages and found an abundance of anaphers, epiphers, alliterations, different types of rhymes, word repetitions, onomatopoetic words, and a great variety of different sentence structures, which are too numerous to be listed here.

4. On the *trobairitz* (female troubadours) see Bogin 1976. On Hildegard see Henry 1983, 16. On women writers see Shahar 1983, 165–173; Petroff 1994.

5. Regarding the male writers' dependence on their patrons, see Bunke 1979, 68–73.

The prologue already provides basic information about the content of the following forty-six chapters and the prologue's own intended function. The book is a "messenger," sent to strengthen *geistliche luten* (spiritual people) in their distress. They are the "pillars" of the church; without them, the church would collapse. Mechthild emphasizes herself as the exclusive source of her books' revelations: "it [the book] refers to me alone, and announces my secret in order to praise [God]. All who wish to understand this book should read it nine times."

Reading as Mimetic Exercise

Underlying this advice to read the book nine times is an unusual understanding of the reading process, which offers clues to Mechthild's spiritual pedagogy. Her secret is obviously not revealed by comprehending words and grammar at face value. What then is the advantage of such repetitious reading? If we look at the text itself, it is striking how often the author implied and evoked repetition. Parallelism is emphasized as the major literary tool; next in importance is the accumulation of adjectives, nouns, or verbs in invocations. Alliteration and anaphora also occur with surprising frequency (Zinter 1931). Heinz Tillmann captures the effect of Mechthild's style when he writes of the "enormous dynamics" of these techniques, attributing to them the "solemnity of a magic spell" (Tillmann 1933, 36). In analyzing her prayers as a form of rhythmic prose, he again points out that they display the same stylistic principles as spells (1933, 41). Medieval spells and healing formulas in Germany share a number of formal structures: end rhyme, strict parallelism, consonance of corresponding terms, and rhythmic character. But the similarity between the almost hypnotic effects of the *Flowing Light* and the chanting rhythms of spells goes even further: the desired effect of the spell is in many cases evoked by repetitious incantation, usually three times (Fehrle 1926, 14, 21, 28). We cannot propose with certainty, however, that Mechthild consciously chose the concept of spells as one of the underlying literary and spiritual principles of her work.[6] Furthermore, liturgical language operates often with the same principles. Yet what both types of speech have in common is the intention to affect the consciousness of the reader and to change her relationship to reality by an influx of sacred "energy" channeled through the spell on liturgical chant. Similarly, a repetitious reading of Mechthild's text has a mimetic function; it creates a psychological reality that duplicates Mechthild's ecstatic experiences. Poetic techniques such as hypnotic rhythm and alliteration had an even greater effect upon Mechthild's audience than they have for readers today because medieval people usually read their texts aloud. Oral recitation creates a greater resemblance between the process of speaking—or, in this case, chanting—and the process of reading (Scholz 1980). Interestingly, Mechthild uses an actual curse in book 1, indicating that she was familiar with the practice of

6. See Fehrle 1926. Compare, for example, a spell quoted by Fehrle (1926, 7) with Mechthild's spell in book 1, chapter 8. (Fehrle uses modern German spelling.)

> Nachtmahr, du leilich Tier,
> komme mir in der Nacht nicht hier
> Alle Wasser sollst du durchwaten,
> Alle Bäumchen sollst du abblättern,
> Alle Blümchen sollst du abpflücken.
> Alle Grübchen sollst du auslecken,
> Alle Sträucher sollst du durchkriechen,
> Alle Pfützchen sollst du aussaufen,
> Alle Hälmchen sollst du zählen.
> Komm mir in der Nacht nicht (zum) quälen.

spells. The curse exhibits all rhetorical charateristics of spells, but pagan and Christian magic are brilliantly fused. It is *God* himself who curses; his curse, as in the ancient Hebrew use of the word, is also a blessing.

> I curse you: may your body die,
> your words be destroyed,
> your eyes close.
> May your heart flow,
> your soul rise,
> your body stay behind.
> May your human senses perish
> [and] your spirit stand before the Holy Trinity.
>
> (1, 7)

Mechthild's explanation of the title of her writings underscores her intention to evoke a physiospiritual response in her audience. When Mechthild asks God for a title for her book, he answers, "It shall be called 'A flowing light of my godhead into all the hearts that live without deceit'" (prologue).

Core Concepts of Mystical Transformation: On Angels and the Human Heart

The heart, seat of the vital pneuma in the medieval medical tradition, represents feeling but also a combination of feeling with a kind of commonsense wisdom, as the context will show. The human heart has its counterpart in the heart of God, and communication between God and soul sometimes takes place nonverbally "from heart to heart." As Grete Luers (1926) has pointed out, the heart was a frequently used synecdoche in other German mystical texts, referring to God as well as to the soul and the experience of a *unio mystica;* she cites examples from

Heinrich Seuse (1295–1366), Johannes Tauler (1300–1361), and the circle around Meister Eckhart (1260–1368). For Mechthild the heart as metaphor and synecdoche has much richer connotations than for us today. In book 1 the heart is mentioned ten times after its first appearance in the prologue. Five out of these ten times it can be found in a description of ecstasy. The "flowing" of the heart is one of the preconditions for the ascent of the soul to the Trinity (1, 7). When God and the soul unite like "water and wine," an image taken from the writings of St. Bernard of Clairvaux, God takes the soul into his glowing heart (1, 4).[7] The Divine Bridegroom seduces his bride by showing her his burning heart (1, 29). The greatest gift Mechthild has to offer is her heart's joyfulness; God places this gift in his own divine heart (1, 38–43).

The heart as a metaphor for psychophysically conceived emotion appears in the terms *herzeleit* or *herzensschwere*, both of which denote sadness (1, 26; 1, 28; 1, 46). As wisdom, it appears in the expression "virtues of the heart," *herzeklicher tugenden* or *tugenden dines herzens*. This expression appears in relation to good works, to *Minne* (courtly love), and to ecstasy (1, 36; 1, 37).[8] The

7. The image of the two entities mixing like water and wine is to be found in the text of Bernard of Clairvaux, *De diligendo Deo* 9.28. Note that for Bernard only love and will as aspects of a person merge in this life, not, as Mechthild implies, the whole person: "To love in this way is to become like God. As a drop of water seems to disappear completely in a quantity of wine, taking the wine's flavor and color; as red-hot iron becomes indistinguishable from the glow of fire and its own original form disappears; . . . so, in those who are holy, it is necessary for human affection to dissolve in some ineffable way, and be poured into the will of God" (Evans 1987, 196).

8. The Middle High German term *Minne* has a number of meanings: remembrance; memory; love; pure, religious affection; parental love; friendship; affection; benevolence; sensual love. The verb *minnen* can mean to give a present, to love (religiously, sexually, and as in a friendship). The meaning of memory and remembrance is rejected by

meaning of *herze* in Middle High German comprises inner forces such as "mind," "courage," "psyche," and the innermost of a person (as in the English expression "in one's heart"). If book 1 itself is understood as the transmission of divine "energy" and insight (symbolized as "the flowing light of the Godhead"), the function of repetitiously reading the text is to influence directly the readers' center of *emotional intelligence*.[9] This term is perhaps awkward, but comes closest to the psychological locus of Mechthild's ecstatic theory of transformation.

The feminist philosopher Alison Jaggar has clarified the difference between emotions as social constructs that merely reflect a patriarchal status quo and the kind of emotional intelligence that the metaphor of "flowing light" refers to in the prologue: "[This book] shall be called "A flowing light of my godhead into all the hearts that live without deceit'" (prologue). Emotional intel-

---

Dorothea Wiercinski (1964). She also lists a meaning in the religious realm, in which *Minne* designates a special act of help of the Holy Spirit (seen as *orator* and *advocatus*). In addition, the term has a special significance in juridicial matters: it can mean the amicable settlement of a conflict, the *pax* between a ruler and his people, the legal proceedings as such. It might also depict a present that secures the friendship between two powers, as in the sense of certain fees or tithes. The verb *minnetrinken* denotes a symbolic act of reinforcing existing friendship or as means to secure a relationship that grants full participation in another person's life. In the legal and political context of the word, Mechthild's use of *Minne* as a third force binding together God and soul gains in depth beyond its emotional value. In regard to *herze*, see Pretzel (1982, 20–21). Grete Luers calls *herze* a synecdoche, which expresses the deepest part of a soul when applied to humans, but she does not explain its meaning when used for God (1926, 196–97).

9. Lauri Seppaenen pointed out that the term *flowing love* (*vliessende minne*), part of the "flowing light," is a translation of the Latin term *amor liquidus* or *amor liquefactus*. According to Seppaenen, the St. Trudperter Hohe Lied (ca. 1150–60) and the mystical encyclopedist Maximilian von der Sandt (Sandaeus, 1578–1656) understood the term as exclusively mystical, whereas Mechthild used it both mystically and ascetically (Seppaenen 1967, 109, 129, 136, 137, 139, 145).

ligence that can see reality beyond the ideological function of conditioned and habitual emotional responses
("hearts that live without deceit") is named "outlaw emotions" by Jaggar. These outlaw emotions represent an
epistemological privilege of the oppressed: "The perspective on reality available from the standpoint of the oppressed offers a less partial and distorted and therefore
more reliable view" (Jaggar 1989, 162). Given Mechthild's
precarious situation, her religiously motivated insistence
on a special kind of knowing becomes all the more poig-
nant when read from Jaggar's point of view.

If we approach Mechthild's work as a manual of ecstatic transformation, the symbolism of a ninefold reading becomes more meaningful. Like other medieval
authors, Mechthild uses symbolic numbers frequently.
The number nine appears most conspicuously in reference to the activities and ontological status of the nine
angelic choirs.[10]

10. On number symbolism in medieval writing see Hopper 1969.
Hans-Georg Kemper suggests that Mechthild uses her biographical
data symbolically. "Allegorische Allegorese. Zur Bildlichkeit und
Struktur mystischer Literatur (Mechthild von Magdeburg und Angelus Silesius)" 1979, 90–126. For example, the twelfth year, in which
she received the first greeting by the Holy Spirit probably refers to the
twelve-year-old Jesus, who discussed matters of faith in the temple.
Kemper also suggests that the number of chapters and books might
have been chosen deliberately; the forty-six chapters of book 1 for example might refer to the forty-six years it took to build the temple of
Solomon (John 2: 20). Kemper mentions the mysterious nine times of
repetitious reading but suggests no interpretation. He admits that
without a concrete relation to the next, the symbolic references remain
speculative and of no consequence. I agree with Kemper. Evidence for
the symbolism of the number nine is, however, much greater than, for
example, the evidence for a possible symbolic meaning of the number
forty-six. Although the idea is intriguing and might refer indirectly to
the Song of Songs, I could find no direct or at least logical relation of
the text in John 2: 20 to a possible decoding of Mechthild's (or her
editor's?) choice of exactly forty-six chapters in book 1 (see Kemper
1979, p. 113, 114 n. 26).

Angels are of some concern to Mechthild. She was particularly interested in the ontological differences between humans and angels. She often compared the human soul to angels, especially to the seraphim. Angelic beings functioning as guides and teachers have also played a significant role in other women mystics' spiritual growth, perhaps more so than for most male mystics and mystical theologians (Francis of Assisi is a notable exception). They appear at crucial junctures in the spiritual development of the Beguines Hadewijch and Beatrijs of Nazareth (1200–1268); an angel functioned as teacher for Elisabeth of Schönau (1129–1164), and an angel wounded Teresa of Avila (1515–1582), to name just a few of the better known examples. Traditionally, seraphim, together with cherubim and thrones, were imagined to inhabit the first three tiers of the nine choirs, thus living closest to God.

Among Mechthild's angelological predecessors are Pseudo-Dionysius, Bernard of Clairvaux, Bonaventure, and Thomas Aquinas. Medieval tradition followed the angelology of Pseudo-Dionysius, who described them as absorbed in never-ending love and adoration. Angels, determined exclusively by their love for God, are a model for Mechthild's mystical path. In book 1, for example, the nine choirs exalt God for his wisdom, compassion, nobility, and gentle guidance (1, 6). The praise begins with pointing out God's concern for angels and ends with their joy about being elevated above other creatures through his *Minne*. Mechthild admonishes her readers to listen to the angels' glorification of God with "spiritual ears" (*geistlichen oren*), a phrase suggesting that angels prefigure the human experience of God.

In book 3, Mechthild's soul has to pass through the nine choirs in her journey to God, during which she is joined by two angelic guides. When she finally arrives, she is tenderly greeted by a divine embrace and kiss; "In this kiss she was moved to the highest height above all the angels' choirs" (3, 1).

In another ecstatic experience, this superiority is described even more daringly:

> The most splendid angel Jesus Christ
> who hovers high above the Seraphim . . .
> I take [him] in my arms, as small a soul [I am].
> And I eat him and drink him
> And do with him what I want.
> That can never happen to the angels
>
> (2, 22).

Mechthild closes with an irreverent "What do I care what angels feel?". Her invitation to read the book nine times might have referred to a mystical process that was understood ontologically as a path beyond the nine angelic realms.

Mechthild's use of the number nine might have stood for a view that posited human beings in relation to the ones closest in created kin, angels, and highlighted the special status of the soul, who alone is created in the image of God. As such, the soul enjoys the highest privilege. Speaking to the allegorized figure of Contemplation (*vro beschowunge*), the soul reiterates the underlying anthropology of *The Flowing Light of the Godhead:* "You have seen clearly that the seraphim are children of God and yet his servants. [But even] the soul with the least merit is daughter of the Father and sister of the Son and [female] friend of the Holy Spirit and truly a bride of the Holy Trinity" (2, 22).

Ecstasies as Initiation, Exploration, and Transformation

The structure of Mechthild's mysticism has had few interpreters, perhaps in part because her poetic style and the brevity of her individual chapters make any deep probing difficult. Margot Schmidt (1985) has pointed out that Mechthild delineated only aspects of her knowledge, without being precise, to leave room for the free workings of the Holy Spirit. Mechthild's experiences have been interpreted mostly from two perspectives: as types of separation between body and mind or according to the pattern of the *Song of Songs* (Schmidt 1985; Fuehrer, unpub. manuscript).

For example, in a model dealing with the separation between body and mind, Schmidt identifies three stages in the ascension of a soul. Reacting to the impact of the force of divine light, body and soul are gradually separated and purified. Their respective sense organs become sharpened and refined to the point that bodily senses merge to a certain degree with the senses of the soul (Schmidt 1985, 140). This transformation goes hand in hand with a shift in consciousness. In the first stage, Mechthild is in full control of her mental powers and can act intentionally. Because she writes that all her questions and requests are answered, we can assume that this stage is sacerdotal in essence. Mechthild here is the messenger for others. In the second stage, she becomes unable to exercise her mental powers intentionally; a passive, receptive consciousness takes over. Finally, in the third stage, Mechthild goes even beyond receptivity. She loses all sense of individual identity and the consciousness of physicality; instead, she is immersed in indescribable joy, absorbed in the miraculous Trinity, annihilated and separated from herself (Schmidt 1985, 128). Sonja Buholzer traces this process of loss of self through Mechthild's use of metaphors such as melting wax, blossoming flower, and dance with God as guiding partner and minstrel (Buholzer 1988, 37–44; see also Hummel 1989; Pike 1992).

Another model that at least partially unlocks the inner structure of *The Flowing Light of the Godhead* is the

Song of Songs, fused with elements of the Neoplatonic tradition. Here the key movement is the estranged soul's return to the divine source of her being (Fuehrer, unpub. manuscript; Beer 1992). The mystical journey thus would begin with a phase of divine courtship, then moving on to a transformation of the soul, a *mors mystica*, in which the full impact of the divine almost extinguishes any trace of Mechthild's humanity. In a third stage, purification is the response to the experience of the withdrawal of the divine lover. As in the Song of Songs, Mechthild's bride searches unhappily for her bridegroom. Finally, mystical union with the bridegroom is achieved in a state of purity and sanctity.

These two interpretations of Mechthild's core teachings reveal surprisingly different layers of the text. The first model delineates the psychological changes in consciousness of a single actress. The second model, based on the Neoplatonic paradigm of alienation and reunion, focuses on the movements of two beings and their inequality of power. Both models are correct, yet each is incomplete when seen by itself.

Mechthild's mystical teachings are presented in the most succinct fashion in her first book. Here all the themes of religious core experiences are touched upon: death and rebirth, return to the sacred beginning of creation, hierogamy (sacred wedding), the immersion into sacred time, and the encounter with divinity. I suggest that these motifs unfold in three distinguishable frameworks of ecstatic experience. What is crucial here is that these frameworks exist simultaneously, not in a linear fashion as Schmidt and Fuehrer suggest for their respective models.

The *grus* (greeting) given by God is the ecstatic initiation to a deeper dimension of being (see esp. 1, 2–17). The soul is taken up to the heavenly realm, metaphorically presented as a royal court. Here she receives a revelation of divine love that triggers blissful raptures in which the body remains passive and uninvolved.

> When the poor soul arrives at court, she is wise and well-mannered. . . . Oh, how lovingly is she received. So she is silent and desires boundlessly his praise. Then he shows her with great desire his divine heart. It resembles the red gold that burns in a big coal fire. And he places her in his glowing heart. When the high prince and the lowly maidservant embrace in such a manner and are united like water and wine, then she will come to naught and move beyond herself, as if she could not go on any longer. (1, 4)

The second type of ecstatic experience is more cognitively oriented. It appears to be modeled after passages in the Song of Songs in which the lovers praise each other's beauty. This courtship cycle, envisioned to take place at the heavenly court, abounds in nonanthropomorphic imagery to express the beauty and joy of the encounter. Although this cycle does not contain descriptions of ecstatic states, its poetic invocations communicate a state of unmitigated happiness (1, 8–20; 2, 9–10; 2, 17). God's intention in this lovely and loving courtship is to "make the simple soul wise." Loving attentiveness creates wisdom. "Thus God woos the simple soul and makes her wise in his love" (2, 17).

The third identifiable ecstatic model revolves around the strenuous *Minneweg*, the path of love that the soul must learn to master (see esp. 1, 23–44). At its climax is the sexual union between the lovers: "So then happens a blissful silence according to the will of both. He gives himself to her and she gives herself to him. What happens to her only she knows, and with this I comfort myself" (1, 44). The Minneweg is distinct from the *grus*, which is based solely on God's action, and the courting, which involves both lovers. It centers almost exclusively on the soul's moral and spiritual responsibility of "growing up" to become the "true bride" (see esp. 1, 23–44; quo. in 1, 44). As Mechthild points out, in book 1, 2, the Minneweg is an alternative to a monastic lifestyle on the one hand and to academic theological learning on the other (1, 2). Both are criticized as extraneous and digressive. In a dialogue between *Minne* and the soul, these outspoken judgments are passed:

> *Soul.* I am in a holy order, I fast, I abstain from sleep, and I am without capital sin. I am bound enough.
> *Minne.* Of what use is it that one coops a barrel and the wine still leaks? . . . .
> *Soul.* I presumed that if I joined a monastery, I would have risen very high.
> *Minne.* What does it help that one dresses a sleeping man beautifully and presents him choice foods while he is asleep, since he won't eat anyhow? Oh, my love, let yourself be awakened . . .
> *Minne.* Oh my, many a man who excels in learnedness and natural intelligence and common sense will not do that—to dare put himself in the hands of naked *Minne*. Only to the simple and pure who sincerely strive for God in all their actions God lowers himself naturally. (2, 23)

The Minneweg is a path of liberation from attachment: "You should court nothingness, you should flee anything material" (1, 35). In more concrete terms, the psychological task is to "surpass the pain of remorse, the agony of confession, the toil of penance, and love for the world, and the devil's temptation, and the excessive nature of the body and the cursed self-will" (1, 44).

In sum, the *grus* functions as initiation into a new dimension of being, the courtship as a cognitive exploration of this dimension, and the Minneweg as the hard-won transformation of the soul to rest more permanently

in the love of God. Underlying all three modes is an overwhelming trust in the love of God for the soul. God
speaks: "That I love you often is due to my nature, because I am Love. That I love you intensely is due to my
desire, because I yearn to be loved much. That I love you
for a long time is due to my eternity, because I am without end" (1, 24).

Categories of Ecstatic Experience in
Books Two Through Seven

Descriptions of ecstatic states in the remaining six
books add certain aspects to Mechthild's ecstatic teachings in book 1. The bride-bridegroom paradigm plays a
less important role; prevalent are descriptions of physical
sensations, selected biographical material, and reflections
on the absence of intense mystical experiences. The female personification of Minne moves into the foreground
as mediator between soul and God and as the stern
teacher of the soul. As is true for Hadewijch's mysticism,
Minne, often characterized as fire, seems to absorb the
harsh and authoritarian features of the Minneweg that
God cannot contain in his image of lover and benign
father.

In the following pages, I will focus on three themes
that relate the aspects mentioned above to each other:
spiritual crises, nonanthropomorphic imagery, and mystical death. All three themes have already made an appearance in book 1, but they are there subordinated to
the descriptions of the *grus* and the Minneweg.

The Absence of Ecstasies:
Integrating Spiritual Crises

We are fortunate to have biographical fragments that
allow some insight into Mechthild's own spiritual devel-

opment with its achievements as well as times of crisis. Chapter 2 of book 4 in particular contains a surprisingly detailed psychological account for the time between her twelfth and forty-third year. The function of this chapter is to authenticate and defend her teachings as divinely inspired: "I must speak [about myself] in the honor of God and also because of the book's teachings." At the age of twelve, Mechthild wrote, she received God's first "greeting" ("I unworthy sinner was greeted by the Holy Spirit in flowing abundance in my twelfth year"). From then on, she became incapable of committing a major sin. The greeting occurred daily and withdrew her from worldly affairs. Thirty-one years later, at the time when she was actually writing this text, the "greeting" experience was still part of her life. In the beginning, all of her religious knowledge was contained in the day-to-day practice of Christian faith ("cristanen globen"). She emphasizes that she never consciously asked God ("mit willen noch mit geren") for states of consciousness that resulted in "blissful sweetness, in such holy understanding, and in such incomprehensible miracles" (4, 2). Neither did she believe that such powerful experiences could happen to any human being. Her insistence on her ignorance about mystical phenomena in these passages, coupled with a noticeable silence about any human teachers she must have had, underscores her belief in the divine origin of her writing. "Thus this book lovingly proceeded from God and not from human thinking" (4, 2).

As she writes in a later chapter (4, 12), the first phase of ecstatic experiences lasted for eight years, but then her first crisis threw "body and soul" into "such great darkness that I lost understanding and light, and that I lost knowledge about intimacy with God, and the very blessed Minne went also her own way."

A second critical turning point, though of a different nature, appears to have taken place in the last stages of her life: "[God] gave me the gift that is described in this book in three ways: first in great tenderness, then in great intimacy, now with burdensome suffering" (6, 20). Her old age lacks all "shining works" and is "cold as regards graces." It is deprived of the energy of youth, which alone can endure the powers of burning love. In an unusual metaphorical figure, she refers to the Trinity in order to to mark the three phases of her spiritual life on earth. If her childhood is characterized as the companion of the Holy Spirit ("din kintheit wc ein geselline mines heligen geistes"), and her youth as the bride of God's humanity, her physically fragile old age is spent as housewife of God's divinity (7, 3). Another Beguine, Beatrijs of Nazareth, also uses the image of housewife as metaphor for a stage in the mystical journey. For Beatrijs as for Mechthild, being a housewife ("mater familias," *Sixth Degree of Love*) marks a certain completion and deepened knowledge, but it lacks the sadness that permeates Mechthild's image. At the end of Mechthild's long mystical journey, erotic ecstasies are superseded by a deeper understanding of the darkness of human life: "Lord, what do we want to talk about courtship when we thus have lain together in the bed of my pain?" (7, 21).

In her struggle for an explanation and integration of the experience of God's absence, the fundamental issue of her crises, Mechthild employs a number of models. Three of them are rather traditional and explain God's absence theologically, morally, and physically. Mechthild's fourth model, a psychomystical explanation, appears to be more original.

Theologically, Mechthild explains God's absence as a direct response to the Fall. Having forfeited holiness, no human being could ascend to heaven and enjoy the bliss of ecstatic union. The incarnation of the Word finally restored the possibility to experience the divine presence (5, 23).

From a moral perspective, distance from God is

caused by sinful behavior (4, 5). A person will stop the divine flow of love if her heart indulges in "useless thoughts" (5, 26) or if she is too much dominated by her own will (7, 55). Mechthild herself seems to have reached such a degree of immunity against sin (she calls it a "unique gift"), that she was able to enter a state of ecstasy immediately when "vices and pain are offered" (6, 26).

On a third, physical level, God's absence can also be experienced as a natural "cooling" process after the ecstatic trance is over. The soul, poetically described by Mechthild in analogy to the sun, rises up in flames, but when it is so intensely enraptured that it swoons, God induces it sink down into the "night," just as the sun cools and descends in the evening (5, 4).[11] A distance from God thus can be part of a natural ecstatic cycle. Because the body can tolerate only a certain amount of intense unitive states, God withdraws voluntarily in order to keep it alive: "[Even if] I touch you very tenderly, I cause you endless pain in your body; should I give myself to you at all times according to your desire, I should dispense with my sweet earthly lodging in you" (2, 25; see also, for example, 5, 29).

These three models, however, do not suffice to explain Mechthild's major personal crisis that afflicted her

11. On the notion of "sinking love" see Seppaenen 1967, 99. Seppaenen understands Mechthild's sinking love in the context of Richard of St. Victor's *amor defectum afferens:* the desire for the object of love, God, grows with the amount of love felt but, as a consequence, the beloved moves further and further away. The human lover becomes humble, and in this humility, the soul sinks down like liquified metal (see Richard of St. Victor, *De quatuor gradibus violentae charitatis,* PL 196, 1222). Alois M. Haas (1979) interprets the notion of sinking love as the reversal of the mystical ascent as presented in the Platonic tradition of Bernard of Clairvaux or the Victorines (115), which ultimately functions as supreme doxology: even in the Fall, in the distance, God can be praised (118). See also Schmidt 1985, 139 and passim.

eight years after the beginning of her mystical experiences. In a dramatic narrative in book 4, Mechthild de-
velops a theory of "sinking love" that has as its
cornerstone the problem of separation between lover and
beloved. As Grete Luers has shown, the mystical term
versenken has been also used by later German mystics
such as Meister Eckhart, Johannes Tauler, and Heinrich
Seuse, but with its opposite meaning. Here "sinking" denotes a process of merging with the divine, not one of
"sinking away" (Luers 1926, 290–91).

In Mechthild's text the soul is depicted as the agent
who, motivated by humility (*demuetikeit*) and love, consciously rejects being raised up to God. It asks God to be
allowed to "sink down"; the crucial momentum here is
the human decision to take responsibility for the distanc-
ing. This self-imposed fall, pushing her into temptations
and the threat of disbelief, results in a paradoxical affirmation: "O blissful distance from God, how lovingly am I
connected with you! You strengthen my will in pain and
make dear the difficult long waiting in this poor body" (4,
12). This attitude, reminiscent of Job, finally triumphs in
the experience so that the deeper Mechthild sinks away
from God, the sweeter and more miraculous her reunions
with God become (4, 12). Rather than fighting periods of
spiritual emptiness, Mechthild accepts them as valuable
opportunities for spiritual growth.

But there is also another aspect to her choice to deliberately let go of and, implicitly, give freedom to the object of her desires and the source of her life. Absence can
create an astonishing equality of status between lover
and beloved. By actively embracing God's absence (*ke-
nosis*), the human lover experiences autonomy of the self
in the face of an otherwise all-encompassing other.
Through a successful coping with spiritual crises,
Mechthild learned to free herself from a dependency on
ecstatic communion. The human condition, imperfect

and limited, thus becomes as dignified and meaningful (perhaps even more so because of its realistic and courageous acceptance of pain and loneliness) as the ecstatic state of fusion with the divine. The choice to embrace the whole gamut of spiritual experiences rather than to depend only on the heights of ecstasy affirms and strengthens Mechthild's self. It is certainly a mark of the maturity of her spiritual teachings: "When she has ascended to the highest that can happen to her while she is still connected to her body, and sunk down into the greatest depth that she can find, then she is fully grown in virtues and holiness. Then she must be adored with the pain of long waiting" (5, 4).

"Quilting" the Ecstatic Themes of Greeting, *Minneweg*, and Courtship

Mechthild's genius lies not only in the complexity of her spiritual vision but also in the sheer inexhaustible reservoir of images and models with which she describes mystical experiences. In books 2 to 7, ecstasies are depicted with ever-new variations. These variations are not mutually exclusive nor do they form some sort of hierarchical pattern. Rather, they are interwoven, resembling a subterranean root system without a center amid texts that deal with topics not related to ecstasies. They are elegant clarifications of each other but presented in a manner that can madden a reader who looks for some kind of logical/logocentric system of presentation. In terms of metaphors, most frequently applied are images taken from nature, either organic or inorganic, and terms that denote motion (see Buholzer 1988, on divine *kinesis* and *stasis* in Mechthild's mysticism). In her discussion of Mechthild's use of metaphors related to smell and music, and sense-related images of the bride, Margot Schmidt coined the helpful expression *sensualized transcendence* ("versinnlichte Transzendenz") to capture the richness of the metaphorical language in *The Flowing Light* (Schmidt 1990). The natural, physical world provides the map, the stuff from which ecstasies derive their linguistically communicable memory.

The inorganic natural images are expressed in pairings such as "high-low" (with its motion of "ascent-descent"), water and fire with their verb complements "flowing-burning," and the polarity of "light-darkness." All these terms depend upon sense experiences; only infrequently do we find comments that attempt to link them with theological terminology.[12] Mechthild does not use these pairs in a logocentric pattern but combines the different images freely—for example, fire may flow (7, 34), and water and fire may share the same attributes (6, 22; 5, 1). The source of light and light itself (usually described as "sun") is God: "And the bright sun of my eternal godhead shines on you"(2, 25). Mechthild does not distinguish clearly between the members of the Trinity as light: the Spirit resembles a beam of light (5, 1), and Jesus Christ is filled with "eternal light" (4, 3), whereas the

12. James C. Franklin wrote a study on the symbolism of liquids in Mechthild's work and explored Mechthild's symbolism of the four elements and their qualities as based on Hellenic elemental and cosmological theories. Because it is almost impossible to establish sufficient evidence for such a hypothesis, the ultimate source for her symbolism probably comprises an almost infinite number of cultural, personal, and psychological aspects. For references to her use of the sun as symbol, see, for example, 2, 25; 4, 12; 5, 1; 5, 4. Luers (1926, 180) speculates that this image might represent an archetype from ancient sun religions. Franklin disagrees with my emphasis on images of light and fire; for him, "the preponderance of Mechthild's images for the manifestations of God are images of water rather than of fire" (1978, 75). The issue here seems to be that Mechthild actually merges images and their effects—for example, fire can flow like water. Such images may be based on the conception that light is a substance through which the object of vision can move from itself to the viewer and literally touches the addressee.

godhead shines as a "playful sun" (4, 12). The soul can absorb the light quality of God. Like a golden shield, the soul receives the rays of the divine sun and reflects them (5, 1). The soul is a "vessel of light" (7, 27).

The image of fire is used for the powers of Minne, who acts as a channel or connecting force between the two entities (4, 19). She burns "in the great fire of heaven" (4, 16). She is hot (5, 4) and draws the soul upwards with a fiery flame (6, 19). And the soul can take on Minne's characteristics, just as it can absorb God's light quality. She feels as if she too were in flames: "Immediately my soul begins to burn in the fire of true love for God with such blissful sweetness" (6, 26). "O fire's glow, set me alight!" (2, 3).

The fires of love, a substitute for the fires of purgatory, serve to cleanse the soul of sins (7, 34). The absence of divine love, as noted above, is experienced as cooling (5, 4), be it because of old age (7, 3) or because of sins (3, 23).

The acts of flowing and flying complement each other. God's energy is flowing downward into the soul (4, 2; 4, 5; 6, 22; 7, 55) as water flows from a well (5, 26). "Flowing" and "floating" are indistinguishable characteristics of the Trinity (4,5; 4,12). As burning is linked to the experience of Minne, so flowing is generally associated with the feeling of enjoyment and bliss of both partners. Both burning and flowing are intensely physical experiences; the mystical and the nonmystical realms merge, as Mechthild herself points out (6, 26). "In my kingdom, I will give you sweet mouth-kissing so that all my divinity shall float through your soul" (4, 5). "And flow toward her [Mechthild's soul] with all of your bliss, which you contain within yourself . . . and the sweet lust of love will float from your divine breast through my soul" (5, 35).

The soul responds to the "flowing down" with a "flying upwards." This flight is sometimes represented as a kind of ride on the breath God inhales, an image we also often find in connection with medieval descriptions of the devil (Czerwinski 1993, 321–429). The movement of flying is closely tied to the symbol of a bird. Flying can be impaired—that is, the soul's spiritual strivings corrupted—by a prolonged sojourn on "earth" (7, 61). "Upward" is the movement to heaven, "downward" to earth. The latter can also symbolize the phase of return in a cycle of ecstasy (5, 4).

In stark contrast to the richly metaphoric language Mechthild employs to describe altered states are the simple descriptions she uses when she refers to her body. The physical cooling during an ecstatic cycle is (at least linguistically) unpretentiously "painful" (2, 3). During ecstasy she "comes outside herself," a partially physical occurrence that resembles a near-death experience (2, 3; 3, 24; 4, 3). "She tastes an incomprehensible sweetness that penetrates all her limbs" (2, 19), and embraced by the Trinity, she swoons (5, 4). Other expressions are: to be touched by God's unspeakable sweetness which penetrates body and soul (7, 50), being drunk with love (3, 3), and experiencing sweetest lust in God (3, 13). Because of their plain, demotic character, these terms suggest directness and authenticity of experience as well as the absence of a second-order theological reflection.

In comparison to the imaginistic code of the Song of Songs and theologically oriented interpretations of ecstatic experience, Mechthild's use of nature symbolism and a simple language that delineates bodily phenomena, strikes us today as the most unmediated, original, and perhaps "primal" layer of the body of ecstatic texts. Ecstatic experience appears here to have been captured in its manifestation as "fields of energy" that are in constant flux: everything shines, flows, burns, reflects, floats, rises, falls, merges, dissipates. The clearest explanation of her model can be found in book 5, chapter 1, where she describes these energies as a kind of shifting magnetic fields. The spiritual is physical, not merely an abstract, colorless realm in the world of thought. Divine light shines and flows into the souls who pursue *Minne*, much like a beam of sun pierces through clouds to reach the earth. Devils "fear this so much that they never dare to move through the holy beam."[13] Mechthild then elucidates this theory: devils have been given circumscribed passageways in the air. These passageways become blocked by the beam that connects a saintly soul with God through ecstasy. Conversely, new passageways are opened wherever evil people walk, who by definition radiate evil "energy" (much like the person who possesses an "evil eye"). If devils encounter good people—or good "energy fields," so to speak—they are driven underground and lose their influence. The painted halo of saints is a faint illustration of Mechthild's literally more far-reaching theory of spiritual auras.

Additional categories of ecstatic experiences, tied together in a patchwork pattern, reach from the primal-archetypal to the highly reflective theological, from the physical to the cosmic. The simplest model consists of a brief checklist of four symptoms the presence of which prove that a soul possesses the love of God: (1) growing desire, (2) flowing pain, (3) burning sensations of soul and body, (4) never-ending union, "bound with great watchfulness" (4, 15).

In book 5, chapter 4, Mechthild discussed the same phenomena, but with a shift in perspective. Physiological reality as point of reference is replaced by the workings

13. The great vision of hell in 3, 21 describes how, with the devil's inhaling, all sodomites are sucked into his belly and are expulsed again when he coughs; God's breath works like a magnet (5, 33). Other examples of the efficaciousness of breath are 4, 12; 6, 13; 5, 35; 4, 14.

of Lady Minne. Laboring within the soul, she enlightens it, teaches the senses, and provides "full strength" ("volle maht") to the virtues. Penetrating through the senses, Minne "storms with all virtues into the soul." She "grows" ("wahset") in the soul and the soul "rises upward to God with longing." Coming full circle, *Minne* then melts from within the soul back into the senses, thereby granting the body its share. This "share" implies a transformation triggered by Minne's force. If we contrast the checklist of the four signs of divine love with the complex workings of Lady Minne, we may conclude that in some ways divine love provides the raw material, primal and powerful, which is modified and dispersed throughout the different faculties within a person by the workings of Lady Minne.

Yet another ecstatic model, a commentary on Paul's notion of three heavens, appears in the context of an allegorical dialogue with "Lady Understanding" (2, 19). Here, Mechthild synthesizes personal experience with an already given theological mold. Great stress is put on the problem of "false" ecstatic experiences. According to Mechthild's exegesis of Paul, the three "heavens" symbolize three dimensions of experience open to the soul. The first or lowest mystical "heaven" is inhabited by Lucifer. Here sad thoughts move in a closed circle, and the soul feels immobilized. It receives no comfort; the senses are victims of illusions. The devil shows himself as a bright angel, even displaying the five wounds (2, 19). In this realm "heaven," made of illusion and sadness, is a parody of true spirituality. The second "heaven" stands for a phase of transition. Although the soul does not yet see God and, lacking proper humility, is still susceptible to the devil, it is able to feel an "incomprehensible sweetness" in all its "limbs." It can hear an (instructive?) voice, but it is colored by earthly concerns. If the soul's humility is perfected, it is allowed to ascend to the third heaven.

Here it receives the "true light" and finally awakens in this "light of open love." Visions and supernatural hearing increase its spiritual knowledge: "Thus she can truly see and understand how God is all in all things" (cf. 1 Cor. 15: 28).

What is most unusual about the third heaven is that ecstasies, otherwise the focal point of Mechthild's mysticism, have no place there. Is this perhaps the result of her attempt to conform to the Pauline tripartite scheme and theological framework? Understanding and ecstatic experience appear together, however, in other books. In book 6, chapter 41, for example, Mechthild states that "bliss, honor, clarity, intimacy, (and) truth" surpass her language capacities, and in book 4, chapter 2, "holy insight" is associated with "blissful sweetness" and "incomprehensible wonders."

Death and Ecstasy

Yet another interpretative approach weaves threads of meaning between life on earth and life after death. Because ecstasies ultimately are experiences of transgressing the boundary between the world of creation and the world of the uncreated creator, they relativize death and the peremptory relationship between body and soul. Most interesting in this model is Mechthild's view on the nature of the souls who are freed from their bodies after death. The soul is imagined as an ideal body, lithe and light, without unsatisfied needs and pains.[14] Blessed souls can drink from the loving flow of the Holy Spirit without interruption (7, 1). Their paradise is to be drunk, to sing out of joy, to laugh "in a well-educated manner,"

14. Although this sounds like a fairy-tale motif, swiftness of movement (*agilitas*) and happiness among the blessed departed are described by Thomas Aquinas and Bonaventure (Weber 1973, 257–63; Stoevesandt 1968, 145–54).

to leap with gracious mien, to flow and swim, fly and climb, and, finally, to move a thousand miles in the time we need to think one thought. A reversal takes place: the lack of a body produces more physical ecstatic joys than the ecstasies of a soul still tied to its earthly companion.

Mechthild's view of mystical death (*mors mystica*) is apparently reflected in references to her own death, which is mentioned most frequently in the first book (which contains her earliest teaching on the path to God and ecstatic states) and the sixth and seventh books, which she wrote at the end of her life. In the seventh book her attention shifts to physical death as result of old age and illness. Unlike the representative of evil forces, the devil, death itself never appears personified but always simply as event, as process, or as threshold to be crossed.[15] In general, Mechthild's images of physical death are never horrifying or fearful (with the exception of the theological "eternal death"). This relaxed attitude is characteristic of the medieval *Tame Death* as Philip Ariès defines it.[16]

15. In European mythology, Death personified enters the stage as the Greek Thanatos, as, for example, in Euripides' *Alcestis*. In Christianity, Death's appearance was dependent upon its grammatical gender: male in Germanic languages, female in Romance languages. A change in Death's appearance in the Middle Ages occurred when in 1300 Pope Boniface VIII forbade the cooking of corpses in order to separate bones and flesh for transport purposes. As a result, Death appeared mummified or as a corpse with a cut in the abdomen, because embalming became the common means of preservation.

16. According to Ariès, "Death . . . is always described in terms whose simplicity contrasts with emotional intensity of the context" (14). Extremely interesting is Ariès' description of the dying person's ability to perform "the last acts of the ceremony" (14): "He begins with a sorrowful and sober recllection of the things and people he has loved and a brief account of his life (14). . . . he asks forgiveness of his friends, takes his leave of them, and commends them to God" (16). In the sixth and seventh book, which was written when Mechthild lived as an old and sick woman in the monastery of Helfta, we find a num-

More complex is Metchthild's *mors mystica* motif, a crucial aspect of her ecstatic spirituality. Her interpretation of the *mors mystica* adds existential depth to her spirituality and puts the rest of her teachings in perspective. This motif is deeply embedded in Christian spirituality; numerous New Testament texts hint at a mystical death experience and the abandonment of individuality. Particularly apposite here are two texts: "I have been crucified with Christ: the life I know live is not my life, but the life which Christ lives in me; and my present bodily life is lived by faith in the Son of God" (Gal. 2: 20) and "I repeat, you died; and now your life lies hidden with Christ in God" (Col. 3: 3).

In the Middle Ages, Bernard of Clairvaux (1090–1153) was among the first to link the *mors mystica* of Galatians 2: 20 and Colossians 3: 3 with the spirituality of the Song of Songs.[17] From his belief in human finitude and the incapability of human beings on earth to see God (cf. John 1: 18; Exod. 33: 20) emerges the concept of a mystical sleep, during which the soul-bride receives her lover, while only her heart is awake.[18] For Bonaventure (ca. 1217–1274), this mystical sleep/death, a perception transcending senses and rational thought, is deeply rooted in a mysticism of the cross (Haas 1979, 406 ff.). Ramon Llull (ca. 1232–1315), however, sees the distance and alienation from love and the beloved as death, while dying *for* the beloved represents for him the ultimate consumma-

---

ber of prayers or litanies that seem to serve the same function (6, 28; 6, 37; 7, 20; 7, 35).

17. In Alois M. Haas (1979, 392–481). the appropriate texts of the Song of Songs are: "If you find my beloved, will you not tell him that I am faint with love?" (5, 8) and "for love is strong as death, passion cruel as the grave; it blazes up like blazing fire, fiercer than any flame" (8, 6). Both verses illustrate well Mechthild's two types of death experience—death as the absence of the lover and death as consummation.

18. The reference for this image is Song of Songs 5: 2, "I sleep but my heart is awake." I could not find this motif in Mechthild.

tion of love. The mystical lover oscillates between life and death: "The lover died because of joy, and he lived because of desire . . . and therefore the lover died and lived at the same time."[19]

Mechthild introduces the term *death* in a variety of contexts, mystical and profane. Applied as a mystical metaphor, it denotes experiences that resemble death in so far as they threaten the annihilation of the self or delineate the extremes of emotional and physical experiences. The most significant example of the latter is the mystical and erotic experience of transcending humanness and immersing the self in the godhead. This mystical event in turn creates a special perspective on death, and it influences to a certain degree Mechthild's nonmystical thanatology. Physical death means nothing but freeing her soul from the body with the promise of eternal mystical states (1, 3). However, we also find a coexistence of traditionally mystical and nonmystical definitions in Mechthild's teachings on ecstatic death. The fact that all these themes are added one to the other without any attempt at logical consistency structurally repeats the unreconciled thematic coexistence of several imaginistic systems in her other descriptions of ecstasy— secular courtly love language, theological discourse, physiological and nature-oriented vocabularies. The Belgian mystic Hadewijch also utilized mixed codes, applying the troubadours' love-death motif in a fashion formally somewhat stricter and more elaborate than Mechthild (see, for example, Guest 1975). Placed in Northrop Frye's framework, Mechthild's work thus represents a transition between the hieratic and demotic code (Frye 1981).

Especially in regard to the link between ecstatic love and death, the overlapping of secular and religious lan-

19. Haas 1979, 411; Llull 1948.

guage is striking. Among the Christian paradigms Mechthild uses are Christ's love-death on the cross (which she imitates in her practice of virtues), the death of martyrs, and, ontologically, the death of the soul as result of the Fall.[20] Her motif of death caused by yearning for the absent lover is a topic in the Song of Songs as well as a standard rhetorical motif in the troubadour lyrics.[21] If the yearning and lonely lover does not perish in a medieval romance, such danger is at least always implied.[22]

The troubadours' imagery of love emerges in Mechthild's words as the soul's pining for God: "O Lord, . . . to see you once as my heart desires and embrace you with my arms . . . what I would suffer for it: no human eye has ever seen it. Yes, a thousand deaths would not be too difficult, so much I painfully long to see you, O Lord!" (3, 23). Death as the consequence of the absence of union, however, accounts only for one aspect of Mechthild's mystical thanatology. Paradoxically, death can also represent a feeling of deepest life and happiness: "In this greeting I wish to die alive" (1, 2) and "this is a sweet complaint: Whoever dies of love should be buried in God" (1, 3).

The spiritual condition of mystics has been characterized as a feeling of utter homelessness, a "sense of be-

20. For Christ's death see, for example, 4, 28; 5, 9; 5, 23; 6, 31; 7, 1. For the deaths of martyrs: 3, 1; 5, 34; 6, 15. For death of the soul: 3, 9; 3, 21; 4, 2; 4, 18; 4, 24; 5, 8; 5, 9; 7, 28.

21. Verses such as the following are typical of the troubadours' vision of death: ". . . in fact this wild desire / Is bound to be my death, no matter if I stay or go" (quo. in de Rougemont 1957, 81).

22. Loomis and Loomis (n. d.): "Tristan and Isolt," 231; "Aucassin and Nicolette," 259; "Sir Orfeo," 317. The motif in Marie de France's, *Les dous Amanz* is retold in Hughes (1943, 11); it appears also in her story "Yonec," in Hughes 71. For German medieval literature see Rehm 1967.

ing lost" in this world (Carse 1980, pt. three, chap. 3; McGinn 1991; see also *The Flowing Light*, 4, 12). A mystic's experience of union and the inherent annihilation of the self is often conceptualized as a return "home" from a life of alienation. Mystics "have a passion to be transformed into something radically different from the familiar terms of earthly existence" (Carse 1980, 69). This transformation "is not . . . from what one is to what one is not, but just the reverse—from what one is not to what one truly is" (69). It is "a passage from a dead present to the eternal origin of life" (80), in whose center lies the rediscovery of one's soul (69). This passage includes traditional mystical concepts such as "alienation—return to true self," physical death as "transition" or "gateway," and "spiritual death"—the separation from the divine source of life—as the only real death. All three themes appear in Mechthild's work. Her feeling of alienation—described as living in a "kitchen" rather than a heavenly court (1, 2)—is symbolized in her need to destroy her inner ties to a profane world. As she admonishes the soul, "you must court nothingness, you must flee whatever exists" (1, 35). A kind of ego death is necessary to experience the mystical *grus:* "this greeting can and must be received by nobody unless he overcame himself and became destroyed" (1, 2).[23]

The "return" to a true state of being, a journey motivated by love (as, for example, in 1, 28) transforms her self and betokens the gift of eternal life. "And love him," Mechthild tells the soul, "so ardently that you could die because of him; then you will burn forever as a living spark in the great fire of the sublime majesty" (1, 28). Psychologically speaking, important here is the sense of

23. Schmidt (Mechthild 1956) relates this quotation to the tradition of negative theology (Pseudo-Dionysius); but see also John 12: 24 (the parable of the grain of wheat) and the list in Luers (1926, 266).

change and movement this inner spiritual journey implies. The soul, still embodied, vacillates between desire
and fulfillment, but also between the different qualities of
intense sense experiences that challenge the integrity and
health of the body: "my body is in great distress, my soul
in high bliss, because she has seen and embraced her
lover with her arms" (1, 5). As in the following quotation,
the body can also be treated with some concern, however: "She [*Minne*] melts through the soul into the senses;
thus the body must also gain its share so that it will be
refined in all things" (5, 4).

Mechthild's experience of mystical death does not
represent nothingness. Death is saturated with love; they
are linked closely in a causal relationship: "Clear Minne
of playful flow causes the soul sweet dismay; she kills her
even without death" (3, 13). During ecstasy, the loving
self extends toward the other to its own outer limit.
Death in ecstasy represents breaking through the barrier
of createdness, the moment when humanness merges
into divinity. This act can appear as cruelty, when Lady
Minne seems intent on destroying the body: "Lady
Minne, you have eaten my flesh and blood" (1, 1). "Tell
me, will I recover from you in the near future? Won't I be
killed by your hand? Then it would be better if I would
have never known you" (1, 3).

God himself can represent this extinction of personhood. Mechthild praises him as "a feast for [my] eyes, a
loss of my self, a storm of my heart, a fall and decline of
my powers, my highest security" (1, 20). A union of both
lovers means a human loss of identity and an experience
close to physical death. "When the high duke and the
young woman of low status embrace each other so affec-
tionately and are united like water and wine, then she
becomes extinguished and loses herself, as if she could
not endure it any longer" (1, 4). Mechthild goes so far as
to state that without the experience of "death," ecstasy is

not complete. "Understanding without enjoyment seems to be the pain of hell for her. Enjoyment without death she cannot complain about sufficiently" (1, 21).

Haas (1979) has suggested that for Mechthild, ecstatic death is a proleptic experience of the nonmystical union of God and soul after death. Death thus turns into an event necessary for initiating this salvific postmortal state. "The experience of bliss caused by God must be described as 'fatal', since, as an event of the other-worldly, [it] is experienced as this-worldly" (Haas 1979, 448; translation mine).

Although Haas's interpretation somewhat neglects the transformatory character of the mystical death experience, it contributes an important aspect to our discussion, namely, the intertwinement of the sacred and the profane that is accomplished by the destruction of physical, bodily reality as a separating wall between the two. Mechthild deepens this fusion theologically by weaving the motif of Christ's suffering and crucifixion into the fabric of ecstatic death. In her interpretation of the creation myth, the Son approves the Holy Spirit's idea to create human beings, but adds, "You know it well, I will die because of love" (3, 9). Earlier the lover seduces the bride by praising his own beauty, but this turns quickly into the prophecy that the bride will have to suffer his martyrdom and crucifixion after the seduction (1, 29). This required mimesis can be performed only through the force of love. The soul will be "wounded by love, dying on the cross in holy steadfastness, your heart pierced by continuous union, . . . ascending to heaven through a breath of God" (1, 29).

In Mechthild's work, ecstatic death affects three dimensions of being. In the first, the earthly, sinful persona has to die in order to free the soul for the union. Complementarily, the absence of the beloved is felt, as in courtly love lyrics, to be another form of death. In the second, death becomes a symbol of physical stress. If ecstatic love would have "no measure, O Lord, how many pure hearts would break in sweet bliss" (5, 4). On the third level, death becomes a symbol of the union between soul and God, the transition to complete, uninterrupted togetherness. As Lady Minne promises, "When your day of Easter arrives and your body receives the blow of death, I will embrace you completely, penetrate you deeply, steal you from your body and give you to your lover. . . . Whoever dies of love should be buried in God" (1, 3).

3

Bliss, Transformation, Values

Ecstasies and Humanistic Psychology

*I*t would be a fascinating task to trace the history of the terms *bliss* and ecstasy from the thirteenth to the twentieth century, much as Jean Delumeau (1978, 1983) has tracked notions of fear and sin throughout the last six centuries. Instead, we are jumping directly from the thirteenth to the second half of the twentieth century, trusting that whatever conceptual changes have occurred in the language games surrounding these two terms can be measured to some degree because of the enduring deep structure of language. Without doubt, our perception of reality is quite different from Mechthild's, but not radically so—otherness and sameness hold a delicate balance that can energize our thinking because it consists of both elements, not just one.

Concepts of bliss and ecstasy moved from background to foreground in the 1960s and 1970s, propelled by larger social impulses that can very well be described as a spiritual renaissance. I suggest that this foregrounding produced a vocabulary that can aid in the understanding and "translation" of medieval mystical models such as Mechthild's into contemporary approaches to spirituality.

During those decades, a renewed interest in the psychology of altered states of consciousness produced a large number of studies that were marked by an appreciation of and a heightened sensitivity to the mystical teachings of Eastern and Western religions.

The research of these decades took three directions.[1] One, focusing exclusively on psychophysiological aspects, neglected to a large degree the "overbelief"[2] of an experience of altered states, and instead concentrated on measuring a shift of consciousness induced by various methods—notably drugs, hypnosis, meditation, and sleep—in clinical experiments. Changes in vital signs such as heartbeat, brainwaves, and body temperature supported the view that states of consciousness are linked to physical phenomena, an observation that many mystics, including Mechthild, had reported (Fischer 1978; see also New Catholic Encyclopedia, 1967, 10: 171–74). With the help of a scientific framework, the reality of mystical experience was freed from being labeled mere idiosyncratic phantasmagoria and validated as worthy of serious consideration.

A second group of researchers, emerging within the movement of humanistic psychology, accepted and integrated certain altered states of consciousness as core elements of personal growth ("self-actualization"). This group attempted to create a system that could classify in particular blissful and ecstatic experiences, the so-called peak-experiences, and link them to specific attitudes, values, and behavior. Traditional mystical experiences

1. This interest, of course, has a history. The founder of the psychology of religion is the German Gustav Theodor Fechner (Elemente der Psychophysik, 1860). Soon, the research of Wilhelm Wundt, William James, E. D. Starbuck, and James H. Leuba followed, but was interrupted by World War I. According to Hjalmar Sunden, (1982), World War II became the watershed between two subsequent phases of research (1920–1939 and 1945–1960).

2. According to Marghanita Laski (1961), this term gained popularity through William James's use in the Varieties of Religious Experiences; it depicts basically "the subjective gloss or interpretation placed by people on their experiences" (1961).

were used selectively as historical examples of aspects of self-actualization. An attempt was made, however, to create a new vocabulary to express ecstatic experiences in a nonreligious, nontraditional way. Although Maslow's value structures and implicit assumptions about human nature in particular have been criticized as reductionistic and even destructive, it is to his credit that humanistic psychology directed attention to the interconnectedness between ecstatic states of consciousness and the formation of spiritual belief systems.

The third approach to altered states of consciousness was more self-consciously syncretistic and religiously oriented. It often embraced the claim of perennial philosophy that one spiritual truth underlies all religious traditions. Thus, Eastern techniques of meditation, trance, and healing were without too many scruples adapted to Western contemporary culture, especially to the spiritual ideals of the sixties. Less accessible but therefore all the more fascinating religious traditions or practices like Sufism, Native American Indian vision-questing, and Celtic druidism were believed to express fundamentally the same religious truth as, for example, medieval Christian mysticism. In general, this movement was more interested in finding a language to express and experience its own historical situation than to become involved in true interreligious dialogue. Self-critical theoretical questions about the similarities and differences between the traditional religious systems and its own perspective were largely avoided. Despite its shortcomings, this syncretism contributed greatly to the process of resacralizing contemporary Western culture. Not only did it create new possibilities of expressing and channeling emerging spiritual interests, but it also made a broader public aware of spiritual and mystical alternatives within its own Western traditions.

Within the framework of a sociopsychological explanation of holotropic states as a medium for restructuring concepts of reality, it is easy to understand why the sixties fostered a concern with mystical states: they allowed subjects to integrate and formulate radically new social and political configurations.

The following sections contain a discussion of models from the school of humanistic psychology and syncretistic psychotherapeutic approaches that integrate ecstatic holotropic states and allow us to relate them to Mechthild's medieval model. In this context, I am viewing Mechthild's works methodologically as a detailed firsthand account of an intense, lifelong experiment with ecstatic states of consciousness in a particular grid of ideological, historical, and biographical coordinates.

I am aware of the limitations of such an interdisciplinary and transcultural enterprise, but it seems that the amount of data and interpretive material now available both in the field of transpersonal psychologies and in the study of mysticism demands an interdisciplinary approach. To avoid overgeneralizations and excessive length of analysis, it is perhaps best to begin such interdisciplinary work with a specific case study.

In the preceding chapters, Mechthild's understanding of ecstasy has been described as a multicentered, multilayered transformatory process through which the human self can evolve to a morally higher, more authentic, and more intense state of being. It has also been described as an initiatory process that vacillates between the psychophysiological experiences of greatly satisfying eroticized pleasure (as in the *grus* and in the *mors mystica*) and the destruction of self-concepts experienced as limiting and habituated ways of being. The experiential dimension of ecstasies is structured by spiritual values such as the preeminence of dialogical interaction and intimacy between the divine and the human, or the soul's unconditional surrender to passionate Love. The intrapsychic process of ecstasies is externalized in an understanding of reality that is fundamentally bipolar (the "higher" spiritual realm versus the "lower" spatiotemporal realm) and dynamic (consisting of fields of positive/divine and negative/devilish "energy" that can "flow," "pull," "attract," etc.). As I will show, a two-tiered model of human existence and a dynamic understanding of intrapsychic reality also mark the philosophies of humanistic psychology and syncretistic psychotherapy; the medieval and contemporary models share at least this one fundamental approach to reality.

The following section will trace the relationship between experiences of bliss, transformation of the self, and spiritual ideals in the works of two key representatives of humanistic psychology: the founder of humanistic psychology, Abraham Maslow, and the founder of the movement of psychosynthesis, Roberto Assagioli.

Being-Psychology

Abraham H. Maslow began his career as psychologist in experimental psychology. Much of his earliest research was dedicated to the understanding of the formation of dominance hierarchies among monkeys. He found that it was not so much overt physical aggression but a sense of confidence and superiority that characterized the behavior of dominant animals in the group. When Maslow changed to the investigation of human behavior, he applied the concept of dominance behavior in the evaluation of his new research material as well. As early as 1939, he compiled the first scale of typical characteristics of human "high-dominance" behavior.[3] His first article on self-actualization was published in 1950 ("Self-Actu-

3. These characteristics include "good self-confidence, self-assurance, high evaluation of the self, feelings of general capability or superiority, and lack of shyness, timidity, self-consciousness or embarassment" (Monte, 1980, 552).

alizing People: A Study of Psychological Health"). His first book, an extensive discussion of his theory and findings on the characteristics of psychological well-being (*Toward a Psychology of Being*), was published in 1962. Until his premature death in 1970, Maslow continuously refined and partially revised his theories. One of his later theoretical essays, *Religions, Values, and Peak-Experiences* (1970) is of particular interest to my study.

Maslow's great contribution to modern personality theory is his attempt to find criteria of mental health and well-being and to develop a system to describe the values, attitudes, and experiences of integrated, healthy personalities. In his view, every human being possesses an "essential inner nature," which can be either developed or stifled in the course of a lifetime.[4] Maslow called the process of accepting and expressing this inner nature "self-actualization."

Although Maslow defined self-actualization in various ways, all definitions are fundamentally consistent with each other. All (a) assume the existence of an inner core or self and the actualization of its latent capacities and potentialities and (b) imply "minimal presence of ill health, neurosis, psychosis, of loss or diminution of the basic human and personal capacities" (1968, 197). Maslow claimed the existence of two qualitatively different but interdependent and equally important psychological dimensions: one governed by the dynamics of fundamental needs necessary for psychic well-being, their satisfac-

4. This is how Maslow defines the human core: "We have, each one of us, an essential inner nature which is instinctoid, intrinsic, given, "natural," i.e., with an appreciable hereditary determinant, and which tends strongly to persist. . . . I include in this essential inner nature instinctoid basic needs, capacities, talents, anatomical equipment, physiological or temperamental balances, prenatal and natal injuries, and traumata to the neonate. . . . These are potentialities, not final actualizations" (Maslow 1968, 190).

tion or frustration; and one organized around the "farther reaches of human nature" (a term that also became the title of one of his books). To achieve full self-actualization, an individual first has to satisfy basic needs ("Deficiency-needs" or "D-needs") such as protection and security, belongingness, self-respect, and freedom in order to develop her capacities and talents (1968, 199, 200). The talents and capacities that can emerge from the "essential inner nature" once our basic needs are met do not appear as dispensable character traits but represent needs as well ("Being-needs" or "B-needs"), because they "press to function and express themselves and to be used and exercised. . . . capacities clamor to be used, and cease their clamor only when they are well used. That is, capacities are also needs. Not only is it fun to use our capacities, but it is also necessary for growth" (1968, 201).

The characteristics of the second dimension, the "Being-state" or "B-state," which is creativity- rather than need-oriented, are expressed in specific values (Being-values), types of cognition (Being-cognition), and experiences (peak-experiences).

According to Maslow, "B-values" are intrinsic attributes of reality. They must be distinguished from the attitude of a self-actualizing person toward this perceived reality such as awe, humility, wonder, reverence, joy, and fear. "Reality" for Maslow thus is essentially meaningful and spiritual. The "B-values" include, for example, truth, goodness, justice, playfulness, beauty, and wholeness (1968, 83; 1970, 93, 94). This emphasis on an exclusively positive pattern of depth reality may be criticized as ultimately destructive and therapeutically counterproductive because it denies the existential validity and reality of painful experiences and suffering. However, it must be noted that, although B-cognition is always part of a peak-experience, it may appear without a peak-experience or even in the context of a painful and tragic situation (242). Corroborating Maslow's view, Marghanita Laski found in her study of ecstatic states that ecstasies could occur during desolate states or desolation experiences (1961, 162). The question then arises of how to define the experience of suffering, or, to put it in other words, whether the validation of suffering always excludes an acknowledgment of beauty and love as intrinsic to reality. For Mechthild of Magdeburg at least, a profound acceptance of suffering and the intense experience of beauty and love were not mutually exclusive.

From a study of 190 college students, Maslow isolated eight fundamental characteristics of B-cognition, which he later expanded to nineteen. The first compilation appeared in *Toward a Psychology of Being;* the enlarged version was printed in *The Farther Reaches of Human Nature.*

During a phase of B-cognition, the observer perceives the percept (which can be any kind of object: a person, a landscape, a piece of music) with complete absorption, a nonutilitarian interest (the percept being valid in itself, without any function in relation to the observer), and heightened intensity of sense perception. The experience is judged to be self-validating, good, and desirable.

The enlarged list, which Maslow compiled years later, included additional categories, such as a sense of philosophical humor, a fusion of inner and outer "world," an impression that the perceived object is sacred, and a synchronicity of analytic and holistic perception. Special emphasis was given to the notion of "innocent cognition," a sense of awareness that lacks and transcends all self-consciousness during the act of perception. "This is all related to my conception of the creative personality as one who is totally here-now, one who lives without the future or past. Another way of saying this is: 'The creative person is an innocent.' An innocent could be defined as a grown person who can still perceive, or think, or react like a child. It is this innocence that is recovered in the 'second naïveté'" (1971, 254).

Peak-experiences, the third crucial element of Maslow's system, resemble closely the descriptions of ecstasies in Mechthild's work. Maslow defined them as complex events that fuse physiological processes with cognitive insights. They are defined as "acute identity-experiences," supremely revealing and expressing a person's "essential inner nature." In *Toward a Psychology of Being*, Maslow offers the following characteristics of peak-experiences [I follow Maslow in the use of the masculine pronoun]:

1. The experiencer feels more integrated than at other times; different psychological functions appear to work in harmony.

2. The experiencer "usually feels himself to be at the peak of his powers, using all his capacities at the best and fullest" (105).

3. The experiencer feels himself more the creating center of his activities and perceptions.

4. His creativity becomes unleashed; he is now most free of fears, inhibitions, blocks, etc.

5. Peak-experiences happen in the "here-and-now"; yet the person becomes more determined by intrapsychic laws than by nonpsychic reality (as far as it is different from the former).

6. Expression becomes more poetic, mythical, and rhapsodic.

7. The experiencer reports often a kind of "B-playfulness" that "could easily be called happy joy, or gay exuberance or delight" (112).

8. The response to peak-experiences is one of feeling grateful and fortunate, because peak-experiences appear unexpectedly and spontaneously.

Peak-experiences happen to everybody, but these "small mystical experiences" (47) are unrecognized and/or repressed in noncreative personalities.

As Maslow pointed out later, peak-experiences are also transient: "They are moments of ecstasy which cannot be bought, cannot be guaranteed, cannot even be sought" (1971, 46). Nevertheless, one can create conditions during which peak-experiences can become more possible than at other times.

Maslow was aware that many if not most of his B-values had often been documented as core elements of intense religious experiences.[5] However, he denied that in contemporary Western culture traditional religious structures were open to the quest of an individual for her authentic self and subsequently to the gamut of peak experiences and B-cognition. In *Religions, Values, and Peak-Experiences,* Maslow severely criticized Western organized religion. Because religious communities tend to resist change, to be anti-intellectual and antiscientific, and to overemphasize piety and obedience, they tend "to produce sheep rather than men" and "become arbitrary and authoritarian" (14). Furthermore, religious communities support a growing split between the sacred and the secular; linking the sacred almost exclusively with the priesthood and its ecclesiastical ceremonies tends to isolate it from "ordinary" daily life. For Maslow, the terms *compartmentalization* and *dichotomization* best characterize the harmful developments of organized religious life.

It is regrettable that Maslow did not address the relationship between hierarchical, authoritarian patterns and the exclusion of women from organized religion. Such an

---

5. It is unfortunate that Maslow was not able to develop his observations in any systematic fashion. What follows is a list of religious ideals that coincided with Maslow's Being-values. "Our description of the actual characteristics of self-actualizing people parallels at many points the ideals urged by religion, e.g., the transcendence of self, the fusion of the true, the good and the beautiful, contribution to others, wisdom, honesty and naturalness, the transcendence of selfish and personal motivations, the giving up of 'lower' desires in favor of 'higher' ones, increased friendliness" (1968, 158). The problem with such a generalized list is, of course, that any religion offers as many proofs as disproofs of Maslow's suggestion.

analysis would have anchored his critique in a more concrete political and socioeconomic context and would have
allowed for a wider applicability of his model.[6] As has
been amply documented in the last fifteen years, the split
between the sacred and the profane, between the orga-
nizers and the organized, traditionally runs along lines of
gender (see, e.g., Ruether 1983). Women's assigned
realm of activity and experience is that of "ordinary"
daily life, and as a group women are still the majority at
the receiving end of mainstream religious organizations.

Maslow's radical alternative to organized religion is
based on the premise that ecstatic experiences, in his
opinion the core and basis of any religion, are natural
and innate to a human being. As such, they precede,
transcend, and question the validity of any temporal social order.[7] Whether interpreted religiously or not, "all
mystical or peak-experiences are the same in their essence and have always been the same, all religions are
the same in their essence and always have been the
same" (1983, 20). This absolutist view is true in so far as
the neurological basis is the same for all mystical experiences, but as cross-cultural research has shown, there are
not only great differences among the types of holotropic
states—the broadest categories being trance, ecstasy, and
vision—but also significant differences in their interpretation and cultivation, because the interpretation of altered
states of consciousness has to be learned (Fischer 1978);
their meaning depends upon the cultural framework

6. See Hooks 1993, for a model of self-actualization that includes
spirituality *and* political action.

7. For a nonfeminist critique of recent changes in the Christian
tradition that links them to values also of concern to humanistic psychology, see, for example, the stimulating presentation of this problem by Donald Capps, who claims that the trend of "an increasingly
close association of religion and narcissism" is redefining both religious tradition and the individual's relation to it (Capps 1985, 242).

available to the visionary or mystic. It appears, though, that in general, ecstatic experiences tend to be perceived as beneficial by religious practitioners if the religious structure in which they occur permits their exploration and cultivation.

Maslow postulated that this claimed sameness and naturalness of ecstatic experiences allowed researchers to equate historical and contemporary reports of ecstasies and to relativize whatever conceptual, cultural, and linguistic framework the particular seer had available in her time (1983, 20). He thus minimized historical and cultural differences. For him, the raison d'être of ecstatic experience unfolds between two symbolic historical moments: a contemporary situation that demands a critical distance from tradition (a claim feminists fully support, if for different reasons) and the moment of birth of a religion that seems to resemble strangely the experience of a twentieth-century self-actualizing person. "The very beginning, the intrinsic core, the essence, the universal nucleus of every known high religion . . . has been the private, lonely, personal illumination, revelation, or ecstasy of some acutely sensitive prophet or seer. . . . these older reports, phrased in terms of supernatural revelation, were, in fact, perfectly natural, human peak-experiences" (1983, 20, 21).

In a commentary on *Religions, Values, and Peak-Experiences*, Maslow revised this somewhat simplistic model and replaced it with the idea that many organized religions develop into two extreme "wings," one mystical and individualized, the other legalistic and organizational. Unfortunately, Maslow never attempted to harmonize his two views or to differentiate the mystical experience of a religious founder from that of a devotee of a "mystical wing." The latter differentiation might have clarified the relation among social status, experience, and interpretative framework because obviously the founder's experience eventually appealed to society at large, whereas the members of a mystical subculture (such as the Beguines) have tended to be comparatively isolated or even actively persecuted.

According to Maslow, a self-actualizing person can integrate these two religious tendencies "easily and automatically" (1971, 331). Nonetheless, ecstatic experiences can pose some dangers: a mystic might seek nothing but peak-experiences and give up any other interest, becoming "not only selfish but also evil" (1971, 332), because he might prefer his own salvation over and against that of others. As a consequence of this exclusive "pleasure-hunt" for ecstasies, an escalation in the use of triggers might occur. Attempting peak-experiences to happen (which is, according to Maslow, impossible), a modern mystic alienated from religious traditions and with no secure place in society might use more and more esoteric, cultish, and destructive methods to reach his goal. This *caveat* contradicts Maslow's earlier insistence on the altruistic value structures intrinsic in peak-experiences; within Maslow's framework, it remains unclear how generally positive Being-experiences can produce egocentric and destructive attitudes. What Maslow seems to point to is a class of pleasurable experiences that resemble peak-experiences only physiologically, but not in its full *gestalt*, which includes a positive value dimension. We are reminded here of Mechthild of Magdeburg's notion of the "second heaven" (66), which describes ecstatic feelings devoid of anything resembling ultimate concerns.

Maslow also eventually rejected his former emphasis on the individualistic nature of the self-actualizing person. He realized that to live constructively in a community and be accepted by it is a paramount criterion for inner growth. Maslow affirmed that all basic human needs "can be fulfilled only by and through other human beings, i.e., society" (1971, 335). Unfortunately, Maslow did not live long enough to work on the political implications and applications of this new, sociopolitical shift of emphasis.

Psychosynthesis

Another representative of humanistic psychology, the Italian psychoanalyst Roberto Assagioli, charted a psychospiritual map of human growth that incorporated a psychoanalytic perspective. Unlike Maslow's behavioristically oriented model, Assagioli's model stressed the importance of the unconscious and conscious, the process of sublimation, and the central role of therapy in uncovering and stimulating psychic dynamics. In 1910 he began to formulate the process of "psychosynthesis," understood as the unification and enhancement of disjointed and underdeveloped aspects of the psyche. His book *Psychosynthesis,* a collection of writings that provides the most comprehensive view of his perspective, was first published in the United States in 1965. By 1981 it had been reprinted twelve times. Because of the methodologically diverse nature of Assagioli's therapeutic growth-model, psychosynthesis shares a number of elements with contemporary feminist spirituality. When it is appropriate, I will briefly point to overlapping characteristics.

Important contributors to the theory of psychosynthesis were William James (from whom Assagioli borrowed the notion of "stream of consciousness"), existential psychology (with its focus on will), and Carl Gustav Jung (for his concept of the four functions of the psyche and the archetypes) (Assagioli, 1981, 3–16). The goal of psychosynthesis is a consciously sought-for re-creation of personality, conceived as the discovery and development of a "Higher Self" (a construct similar to Jung's ideal of the

Self). Like Maslow, Assagioli suggested two qualitatively different phases of self-actualization; the more elementary stage of psychosynthesis he called "personal" and the more advanced "spiritual."

Assagioli assumed that the field of "Unconsciousness" (our ordinary waking awareness) is embedded in a sphere of four different types of the unconscious, which could be imagined as forming separate but permeable layers above and underneath it (1981, 17). The Lower Unconscious serves as the deposit of pathological drives (phobias, obsessions, etc.), uncontrolled parapsychological processes, complexes, fundamental drives, and primitive urges (this resembles somewhat Maslow's dimension of "deficiency-needs"), and the coordination of physical functions. The Middle Unconscious is defined as the reservoir of preconscious material, which is prepared to enter normal waking consciousness; it consists of "ordinary mental and imaginative activities" (17). The third layer is called the Higher Unconscious or Superconscious. According to Assagioli, "from this region we receive our higher intuitions and inspirations—artistic, philosophical or scientific, ethical 'imperatives' and urges to humanitarian and heroic action. It is the source of the higher feelings, such as altruistic love, of genius and of the states of contemplation, illumination, and ecstasy. In this realm are latent the higher psychic functions and spiritual energies" (17–18). In psychosynthesis, the Conscious Self or "I" is expected to "awaken" to its "higher" or "true" Self, which is ultimately not a second, different, self but a more integrated form of consciousness and knowledge that emerges from the Superconscious.

The last layer is the Collective Unconscious, a concept Assagioli borrowed from C. G. Jung. In postulating a Collective Unconscious, Assagioli stressed the deep interconnectedness of human beings, a claim Maslow began to formulate only gradually in his research.

Psychosynthesis complements to a certain degree Maslow's self-actualization process. Maslow, although using the term "self-actualization," gave very little attention to the inner workings of the psyche. True to his background as experimental psychologist, he isolated "higher values" and types of cognition and experience and granted them a certain independence and autonomy from the self. Because of his training as psychoanalyst, Assagioli's attention, however, became focused on the individual psyche as the source of behavior, feeling, and attitudes.

What both share, however, is the fundamental premise of personal growth, of the superiority of experience over theory (as, for example, in regard to organized religion), and of the reality and desirability of health. However, both, seemingly unaware of their racial- and gender-specific assumptions, share an implicit bias toward a white androcentric world-view. An implicit androcentric ideology emerges in Assagioli's system, for example, in his separation of "personal" and "spiritual" realms, in which the "personal" is generally assigned the "lower" value; in his emphasis on the capacity to control one's emotions and "lower instincts"; and in his insistence on a hierarchically ordered unconscious in which the "higher" unconscious is ultimately superior to the "lower." In the history of patriarchal dualism, "lower," "personal," "unruly," and "emotional" have been judged to be negative and have been associated with the "feminine"—that is, with all groups that defied "masculine" stereotypes (women, people of color, gays, and men who reject the status quo). Values such as "higher," "spiritual," "controlled," and "mental" have been construed as superior and "masculine."

To his clients Assagioli offered a number of techniques that promised the achievement of personal psychosynthesis. The successful completion of this process is marked by four features:

1. Thorough knowledge of one's personality
2. Control of its various elements
3. Realization of one's true self—the discovery or creation of a unifying center
4. Psychosynthesis: the formation or reconstruction of the personality around the new center (1981, 21).

The task of knowing oneself imitates the therapeutic process in psychoanalysis, in which clients confront and work through painful aspects of their inner lives such as fears, conflicts, and repressed memories. This step also reverberates with the Jungian encounter of the "shadow." However, Assagioli differs from both psychoanalytically oriented introspection and Jungian shadow work in trying to uncover those positive forces he believed were hidden in the vast landscape of the unconscious and formed an intrinsic part of the psyche.

In a second step, psychosynthesis attempts to strengthen the client's will, which is seen as an "essential function of the self" (1981, 5). Using the will as a tool, a client is encouraged to purge the self of wrong identifications with "a weakness, a fault, a fear or any personal emotion or drive, . . . [with which] we limit and paralyze ourselves" (1981, 22) and then to identify with positive and desirable character traits.

Although Assagioli conceded that the realization of one's true self can take place through spontaneously occurring inner growth, he recommended the use of psychospiritual techniques for spiritual psychosynthesis. These techniques aim at three goals:

1. The transformation, sublimation, and redirection of psychic energies
2. The strengthening and maturing of weak and undeveloped functions
3. The activation of superconscious energies and latent potentialities (1981, 6).

It is interesting that all of these elements are used in feminist/womanist spirituality (Mariechild 1981; Iglehart 1983; Morton 1985; Starhawk 1987; Townes 1993), but with one important difference. From a feminist/womanist perspective, the acknowledgment of fears, painful memories, and self-destructive adherence to negative values and assumptions is turned into a trenchant statement about the harm done to women in a patriarchal society. The use of personal will is sometimes understood as the efficacious principle of "magic"; magic in feminist wicca spirituality is defined as the power to change both personal and collective consciousness. It is a political act in so far as it is geared not just toward personal goals, but also toward changing society to make it a better place for individuals (Starhawk 1987). In Assagioli's model, the political dimension of personal growth, however, is missing. As such, it counteracts possibly liberating effects of psychosynthesis.

Phase two in Assagioli's system, spiritual psychosynthesis, can be reached by a great variety of techniques, including visual imagery, meditation, symbol utilization, self-criticism, and emotional catharsis. Unlike Maslow, Assagioli assumes that individual spiritual psychosynthesis is part of a cosmic scheme, of which "spirituality" in the traditional sense is only one aspect. From Assagioli's perspective, "spirituality" includes all forms of *awareness* that possess idealistic (vaguely defined as "higher than average" [1981, 39]) values, be they ethical, aesthetical, humanitarian, or altruistic. Spiritual needs are claimed to be as basic as material needs (193). Spiritual psychosynthesis is not, as in Maslow's system, an isolated achievement of superior individuals, but "the individual expression of a wider principle, of a general law of inter-individual and cosmic synthesis: . . . Each and all are included in and part of the spiritual super-individual Reality" (30–31). This supreme reality, whether conceptualized as a divine being or a cosmic energy, works within all toward "order, harmony, and beauty, uniting all beings . . . with each other through links of love" (31). What everyone may achieve on a personal level is repeated on a cosmic scale, "slowly and silently, but powerfully and irresistibly" (31). Assagioli called this process "Supreme Synthesis" (31). However, he refrained from developing this concept into a theological system— maybe wisely so, because his lack of concern for the *religious* and *political* dimension to problems such as evil, death, and illness would expose the one-dimensionality of his ontological optimism; he interprets "negative emotions" such as fear, hatred, or the urge to hurt, as attitudinal problems that can be changed on an individual basis. Reducing the problem of evil to personal behavior bars access to a more complex analysis that can posit the individual in a larger historical and theological context (Townes 1993).

Assagioli's self-imposed constraint in actually *guiding* his self-realizing clients spiritually is more constructive because it endorses religious tolerance and pluralism; psychosynthesis, Assagioli wrote, only "leads to the door" of the great Mystery, "but stops there" (1981, 7). He defines as his purpose the facilitation of the experience of spiritual reality but distinguishes it from a body of theological or metaphysical formulations, which would mold psychosynthesis into yet another sect rather than a school of therapeutic intervention (195). This tolerance for diverse religious convictions, however, is rooted in a problematic assumption that we already encountered in Maslow's work: all spiritual *experiences* are assumed to be fundamentally the same and may find expression through any number of symbols and religious systems (195). But symbols are always polysemous and can express oppressive as well as liberating truths. The ambiguous nature of symbols is particularly obvious in regard to gendered images of the divine. A spiritual experience of the Virgin Mary, for example, can alienate women from their sexuality in a way an experience of Ix-tel or Aphrodite may not, yet all three symbols overlap in manifesting divine reality as female.

According to Assagioli, the experience of the spiritual self is one of freedom, of deep interconnectedness with other Higher Selves and with reality. It is felt to be simultaneously individual and universal. It can be manifested abruptly as in a conversion experience or as in the sudden illumination of awakening in Zen-Buddhism (Assagioli 1981,188). The core of the newly created human self, the "Higher Self," is defined as a *state of consciousness* characterized by "joy, serenity, inner security, a sense of calm power, clear understanding, and radiant love. In its highest aspects it is the realization of essential Being, of communion and identification with the Universal Life" (33). If we read this passage carefully, the values used to describe this ideal self, so intriguing at first glance, reveal an image of human nature that is static ("calm" power rather than dynamic, involved energy, "essential Being" rather than "existential Becoming"), impersonal ("communion and identification with the Universal Life"), and separate ("inner security," undisturbed inwardly centered power). Emphasized are control and power rather than dialogue and openness to change. This ideal is quite different from Mechthild's definition of an ecstatic self, which emphasizes the unpredictability of the encounters between self and divinity, the intricate and ever-changing flow of emotion, the primacy of vulnerability with its promises of insight and growth. Mechthild's view of the ecstatic contrasts with Assagioli's emphasis on aloofness and accepts periods of meaninglessness and helplessness as unavoidable and even possibly spiritual life experiences.

Despite his caution, Assagioli did not completely

abandon the use of religious language. He identified the "Higher Self" with the soul (1981, 86) but recommended that his trainees use terms consistent with the world views of their clients. Relying on Carl Jung, Assagioli suggested two types of symbols for meditation on the Higher Self. One group contains abstract, geometrical, or nature symbols such as the sun or stars or a rose. The other set comprises personifications such as angels, the Old Sage, the Inner Christ, or the Inner Teacher or Master (203). Symbols are also used in the technique of inner dialogue or mimesis between the undeveloped and the Higher Self (Assagioli recommended, for example, the myth of the Holy Grail or Dante's *Divine Comedy* as scripts for mimetic exercises), but their choice depends on the background of a client. As an historical example for the technique of inner dialogue, Assagioli mentioned *The Imitation of Christ* by the German mystic Thomas à Kempis (206).

In regard to holotropic states of consciousness, Assagioli, like Maslow, accepts them as valid and somewhat constructive, because they may influence inner reality and outer behavior. As such, they are real (Assagioli 1981, 196). A mystical experience, narrowly defined as "union of love with God, a state of spiritual ecstasy accompanied by bliss, self-forgetfulness, and a forgetting of all outer reality and environment" (207) is, however, not as central to Assagioli's thought as the peak-experience is to Maslow's theory. Assagioli does not emphasize the cognitive element in such experiences; ecstasies are defined as pleasurable physiospiritual episodes with little consequence. This almost casual treatment of ecstasies fits into Assagioli's overall design. The ultimate nature of spiritual psychosynthesis is extroverted in that its supreme goal is an increase in creativity and the dedication to "give of oneself" in whatever field of *work* one feels drawn to (207). A mystical experience, defined in Assagioli's narrow sense, represents at most a stage in learning to contact and manifest the consciousness of the Higher Self, but it is by no means mandatory. Assagioli's psychology is, in comparison to Maslow's, less ecstatic than achievement-oriented in outlook. What it adds, however, is a consideration of the importance of symbols, consciousness-changing techniques, and a more complex model of the human psyche.

The Approach to Ecstasies in the Works of Mechthild of Magdeburg, Abraham Maslow, and Roberto Assagioli: A Comparison

One of the most remarkable and later on often neglected aspects of Maslow's research had been his effort constantly to enlarge, refine, and revise his vision of psychic health. Notes on the tentativeness of all his findings and a persistent anxiety because of the lack of traditional theoretical support for his often intuitive insights permeate all his writings and present the picture of a self-reflective researcher who is personally deeply involved in his work, though isolated from the mainstream paradigms of his field.

In contrast, Mechthild could draw from a richly developed religious tradition that accepted altered states of consciousness as part of human nature, expressions whose validity was accepted by both religious specialists and ordinary people alike. She was able to endow her ecstasies with culturally accepted meaning: that is, she could creatively and meaningfully relate them to a wide variety of issues, including her personal life, her society, her friends and enemies. Her religious tradition was still flexible enough to allow her personal views to become social and public statements (at least to a certain, precarious degree). The contrast between prevailing main-

stream paradigms of the time and Mechthild's personal
views was, though strained, less radical than the contrast
between Maslow's status as outsider and originator of a
new model (his emphasis on psychic health) and his peer
group of traditional psychologists (working with models
based on studies in psychopathology).

If we compare Mechthild's teachings with Assagioli's
approach, we find that like the Italian psychotherapist,
Mechthild intended her writings as instructions for
others rather than objective descriptions of experiences.
But although the suggestions of how to follow the path of
Minne functionally resemble to a certain degree psychosynthesis therapy, Mechthild was not interested in guiding her "clients" toward a purified and neatly organized
consciousness—a "Higher Self"—as deterministically as
Assagioli. Her experiences were intended to set an example; nonetheless, her teachings stress individual response, not mere imitation. Neither does she subscribe to
the vision of a single, unified self that has successfully
and once and for all erased any "lower" drives and incli-
nations. Her self is complex and decentered, and its rul-
ing principle is that of struggle and dynamic interaction,
most clearly exemplified in her lively allegorical dialogues. Tensions between the different centers of the human self, and the self and its environment, do not end
until death, and the outcome of these struggles reaches
even beyond death. The desire for change and the passion for a more intense and unified vision of existence
can certainly be detected in both Assagioli and Mechthild; Mechthild, however, seems more tolerant and accepting of the enduring nature of human weakness.

Mechthild's heuristic approach differs strongly from
both Assagioli's and Maslow's. All her teachings, like
those of many other medieval mystics, are the result of
an intense and intimate involvement in the subject of her
interest. She can teach with the authority and authen-

ticity of someone who has lived and experienced the content of her teachings. In other words, the positivistic split between subject and observed object is noticeably absent in her work. Despite her repeated claim of being merely a mouthpiece for God, her insights are an intriguing mixture of subjective and traditional materials. Like Mechthild, Maslow was very explicit about his personal involvement in studies of human well-being: he wanted to understand those people whom he selected as great examples for his own life. Yet he never completely abandoned his detached position as observer and judge. The traditional scientific paradigm determined at least in this circumstance Maslow's heuristic method. Assagioli is even further remote from a more personal involvement. He defined his role strictly as that of an uninvolved facilitator. This is quite appropriate ethically, because the therapeutic situation demands that therapists refrain as much as possible from gratifying their own ego needs while working with clients. On the other hand, as I indicated above, to refrain from formulating and reflecting upon one's own belief system in encounters with diverse religious belief systems of clients allows unconscious biases to seep into one's work and ossifies authoritarian relationships that model and reinforce political structures outside the therapeutic relationship.

Definitions of Personality
and the Role of Values and Cognition

Maslow's system is rooted in the assumption of an essential inner nature of human beings, which exists for most of us only in a hidden and potential way. A person thus is always more than she appears to be at a given moment. A fundamental trust in the possibility of "personality development" bestows a strong dynamic element on Maslow's notion of personhood.

The "naturalness" of this inner nature can inspire a feeling of sacredness, but to call it such is dependent exclusively on the value judgment of the self-actualizing individual. Maslow refrained from formulating dogmatic definitions of the ontological status of a human being and the character of "nature" (which for him replaced "God" as final cause of humanness). Given the anonymous and impersonal entity "nature" and the flexibility of personality formation, a human being thus finds herself as her own maker, limited only by her range of insight and will.

Mechthild's view of personality operates on the premise of an "inner" self as well, but it is significantly different from Maslow's "inner nature." First, it is not hidden or only rudimentarily developed. Created by God, it is from its birth perfect and fully "self-actualized." Its being cannot be diminished or augmented. Second, like the body, it can only be hurt or healed; human action cannot manipulate its "growth" or "development." Rather, the condition of the soul is determined by the fixed categories of beauty and ugliness, insight and lack of insight, intensity and sluggishness. If a human being adheres to harmful values, the soul will be "stained," hurt, and her beauty destroyed. In contrast, a life lived according to "good" values will clarify and beautify the soul and strengthen her to withstand adverse forces in life. Rather than being exposed to gradual change, the medieval soul can "be" in only one of two states, with no gradual transition between them. Movement happens only within each category: what is beautiful can become more beautiful, what is ugly can increase in ugliness. Mechthild's model is more dialogical than Maslow's: the soul's health is based on the dynamics of intimate love rather than solitary struggle.[8] Third, the soul is not

8. See, for example, 1, 3, and 1, 24 which celebrate the insight that "the more you love me the more beautiful I will become" (1, 2).

"natural" but thoroughly "supernatural." But so is life's potential on earth: the boundaries between the sacred and the profane are not as closed as they are for us today, but flexible and open; the "energies" of the sacred spill into every aspect of life (Czerwinski 1993).

If Maslow's assumption that all peak-experiences are alike is true, then at least some of Mechthild's ecstasies should resemble the definitions given by Maslow, especially because both agree that it is the innermost core of a person that is expressed in ecstasy, be it the "essential inner nature" or the soul. Maslow's experiences are by definition experiences of the self, whereas Mechthild experiences exclusively ecstasies of union, in which a sense of self as separate and unique can be diminished or turn insignificant. Mechthild's ecstasies are therefore not "acute identity-experiences" but rather "acute love-experiences." These experiences, however, give Mechthild an overwhelming sense of self-confidence; her being is affirmed because she feels loved and unconditionally accepted. In the sense that ontogenetically a feeling of identity is established only through loving feedback by others, Mechthild's ecstasies are identity-experiences in a much profounder sense than the solitary peak-experience of a Maslowian self-actualizer. Maslow presupposes that "God" is a matter of subjective interpretation and that "nature" is in contrast an unconscious, unresponsive matrix (a *prima materia*, so to speak), despite the contradictory fact that subjects during B-cognition appear to appreciate any objects of their gaze in an "I-Thou" relationship. These a priori ontological decisions are diametrically opposed to Mechthild's experiences.

Despite such fundamental differences, Mechthild's descriptions of ecstasies coincide with the following Maslowian characteristics. They are transient: "He gives himself to her, and she gives herself to him . . . but this cannot remain for long" (1, 44). Moreover, the response is a feeling of being grateful and fortunate; God encourages the soul: "Praise me for my faithful protection! Thank me for my lavish gift! Desire my holy miracle! Ask for a good end!" (3, 12). Mystical expression is, in addition, so poetical, mythical, and rhapsodic that it seems to have a kind of "Being-playfulness"; Mechthild writes, perhaps tongue in cheek, that the existentially profound encounter with God may look like losing oneself in picking flowers on a meadow: "If this letter [text] is too long, then this has caused it: I had been in the meadow, and found many different flowers" (1, 3). Furthermore, as an experiencer of ecstasies Mechthild appears to be free of fears or inhibitions and feels more integrated than during nonecstatic states. Although conflicts between different parts of her personality (body, senses, reason, and soul) arise before and after ecstasies, a certain conflict resolution is reached during ecstatic states in the sense that the soul is freed from the distracting influence of the other faculties. Mechthild can focus on and live in the presence of what she desires most: the divine. But ecstasies did not always give Mechthild a secure sense of transcendence; sometimes they were too strong for her to endure, especially in old age. Maslow had a similar observation about aging: "I have pointed out elsewhere that the aging body and nervous system is less capable of tolerating a really shaking peak-experience. I would add here that maturing and aging means also some loss of first-timeness, of novelty, of sheer unpreparedness and surprise." (1971, 36).

Maslow's distinction between intrapsychic and extrapsychic reality, which are assumed to merge during peaks, seems to be less helpful as a category. First of all, Mechthild is not interested (as was, for example, the visionary Hildegard of Bingen) in nature and its inherent psychospiritual character. In her poetry a rose is never

valid in itself, but can only serve as synecdoche or metaphor for something else. In regard to changes in perception, however, Maslow's perceptual shifts vis-à-vis
physical reality are to some extent true for Mechthild's
spiritual dimensions symbolized by spatial metaphors.
The ecstatic gestalt is expressed partially as a heavenly
setting and event to which her soul is transferred and of
which it becomes a part. Ontologically different dimensions—earth, heaven, purgatory, hell—remain unmixed
yet meaningfully related to each other as spatial symbols
of psychic reality. For Maslow, on the other hand, what
changes at the point of merging is not a place, but perception per se. Change takes "place" within, not without.
Mechthild projects an extension of psychic horizons;
Maslow introjects it.

For Maslow as well as for Mechthild, values are extremely important, and each distinguishes between
"higher" and "lower" values. I already described Maslow's
D- and B-values; Mechthild differentiates between values
that apply to all humans and special values that become
known to and are understood only by the followers of
her teachings, "spiritual people." Values that Maslow
and Mechthild appear to share (at least approximately,
given the great divide of time) are truth, goodness,
beauty, aliveness, justice, simplicity, and self-sufficiency.
Values that are exclusively Maslowian are wholeness, the
ability to transcend dichotomy, uniqueness, perfection,
necessity, and effortlessness. This list, roughly hewn as it
is, reflects modern affluent sensitivities and social contracts: the split between a private and public persona, a
mass culture that shuns diversity and at the same time
succumbs to a cult of uniqueness, the intolerance for personal imperfection and the denial of the inevitability of
problems, hardship, and evil.

The desirable values that are exclusively Mechthild's
are equally revealing about her culture. Mechthild extols

a willingness to suffer (4, 1); the ability to withstand evil, to mortify and subdue the body (4, 2); the rejection of materialism (4, 7); the destruction of the earthly self (1, 2); the love of God (1, 21) and subjection to his will (1, 27); an indifference to worldly values (1, 27); an indifference to painful emotions and worldly success (1, 32); the rejection of social ties (1, 35); good works (1, 35); and virtuous behavior (1, 35), to name just a few.

This brief comparison indicates that Mechthild's ecstasies have a different relation to a search for well-being than Maslow's peak-experiences. Despite great moments of joy, Mechthild's culture saw earthly life as harsh and demanding and accepted it as such. Mechthild perceived the dangers of succumbing to evil to be greater than Maslow's model acknowledged. Mechthild's moral attitude is more dichotomizing and accusatory than his; in contrast, Maslow continuously attempts to harmonize and unify. Consequently, Mechthild's ecstasies appear as extraordinary and almost exclusive resorts of happiness and peacefulness in an otherwise difficult environment, whereas Maslow champions the idea that self-actualizing persons not only emerge from but have also managed to maintain and/or create a positive and stimulating environment for themselves. From Maslow's perspective, Mechthild's lack of a number of crucial B-values thus could indicate that despite a frequent occurrence of consciously accepted and enjoyed "peak-experiences," Mechthild had not been a truly self-actualizing person. But as the contrast in values has indicated, culture and environment determine to a large degree what are desirable character traits and what are not. The creative unfolding of a self that goes beyond mere survival is heavily dependent upon a benevolent, positively stimulating environment. As Maslow himself pointed out, the conditions of pursuing self-actualization rely on a society's capacity to satisfy an individual's needs, both on a very basic level (providing safety, stability, belongingness, etc.) and on the level of sophisticated creative and psychological functioning. This insight adds a political dimension to Maslow's model, of which he himself was largely unaware.

The medieval values displayed in Mechthild's text appear optimally suited for survival in a difficult environment. Mechthild's religious framework provided an additional dimension to explore and express the creative impulse. Most noteworthy are the capacity to endow suffering with meaning rather than experiencing it as anomic and annihilating, the ability to move beyond the limiting structures of a misogynist society and to create alternative patterns of reality and an alternative sense of self, and the ability to open up new channels of relating constructively to one's environment.

On the basis of these differences, we may modify our previous judgment on whether or not Mechthild was "self-actualizing." Certainly, a medieval mystic could realize select B-values, such as creativity, originality, self-sufficiency, and trust in the efficaciousness of truth, goodness, and beauty. Given Mechthild's brave response to the difficult life as a Beguine and given the fact that Maslow knew only a very small number of truly self-actualized persons and lived in a culture that still discourages ecstatic states (in other words, given that his *theories* were more speculative than indicative of sociocultural reality), the differences in the remaining set of values should be accounted for by the particular historical contexts in which Maslow and Mechthild lived. Against the background of Mechthild's harsh circumstances, her values indicate a remarkable sense of realism. A psychological outlook built on the ability to tolerate difficulties and to acknowledge the inevitability of evil, to be aggressive when necessary, and to believe not in human goodness alone but to trust in an ever-present, transcendent, loving being, appears to be as much an expression of self-actualization as Maslow's range of B-values. Accepting hardship as a substantial part of life, however, affects the integration of peak-experiences as well. For Mechthild ecstasies sometimes deepen the feeling of alienation from "heaven" and heighten the awareness of earthly misery: "O Lord, all your gifts, which I received from you, I experience as painful slaps in the face, because your highest gifts show me to be so low" (4, 5).

It appears that only in a highly developed B-state, embedded in a generally life-enhancing and problem-free environment (the luxury of a chosen few), can peak-experiences be judged as unambiguously rewarding.

Maslow nonetheless did not completely evade the issue of suffering and destructiveness. Especially in his later writings he admitted that certain "pathogenic deprivations" (1971, 308) could seriously hinder growth. He called these blocks *metapathologies*, assumed to be caused by a deprivation of B-values (1971, 305). Although evil appears on his chart of these metapathologies, his gamut of deprivations—from dishonesty to meaninglessness—is merely defined as "illnesses." For Mechthild, however, good and evil are at their core characteristics of God and devil: they are "spiritual," not "natural" values. They can only be imitated (as a mirror reflects an image) and manifested through intentional action. Rather than moving beyond them, any "self-actualization" in her system sharpens the awareness of moral issues. The danger of succumbing to temptations never ends during a life span. "Illnesses," in contrast, are transient. They can be healed and disappear; defining evil as an "illness" implies that it is merely the absence of "health" and promotes the optimistic belief in its "manageability"; Mechthild's medieval position is more pessimistic. Even as a mystic, she cannot heal or master evil, but only avoid and limit it.

Despite the lack of a category for the supernatural quality of Mechthild's "object" during ecstatic cognition, as pointed out above, we recognize some themes of Maslow's B-cognition in Mechthild's ecstatic states. Mechthild as subject becomes self-forgetful: "This greeting can and must not be received by anybody who has not first transcended and annihilated himself" (1, 2). For Mechthild as for Maslow, the experience is self-validating; ecstasies in themselves are recognized as good and desirable. Their possible danger for the body is admitted and deplored. The experience is felt to be sacred. It is true in a much deeper sense, however, that Mechthild's percept receives all the attention of the perceiver and is judged to be "as if it were all there was in the universe, as if it were all of Being" (1968, 74). For Mechthild, God is the ultimate source of her own being and of reality, whereas the objects of Maslow's B-cognition seem merely to represent reality ("nature") but do not appear as source of all reality. Although unique, they are exchangeable: it does not influence the quality of B-cognition whether Maslow's subject is absorbed in looking at a flower or at a child. For the mystic Mechthild, cognition of the "object" God is irreplaceable because of its unique divine quality.

In sum, Maslow's criteria of peak-experiences, B-values, and B-cognition and the gestalt of Mechthild's ecstasies resemble each other in some respects, but differ in others. It has become clear that certain intense experiences—whether they are called ecstasies or peak-experiences—exist as innate human potential but their perception, integration, and utilization is to a large degree culturally dependent. It has been Maslow's great contribution to begin to chart these experiences in contemporary language, but as a comparison with Mechthild's accounts teaches, much needs to be clarified and explored.

In comparing Mechthild's model with that of Assagioli, the concept of a divine being, the relation between self and community, and ecstasies necessitate some comment. Assagioli proposed a single cause for the complex phenomena of psychosynthesis. Instead of God, however, Assagioli preferred the terms "cosmic energy" or "Universal Life." Since this "energy" displays will, love, and constructive behavior, it is more personal and anthropomorphic than Maslow's notion of "nature." "Cosmic energy" thus comes closer to Mechthild's theistic beliefs than Maslow's concept, but it lacks the specific features of medieval affective mysticism. Mechthild, in turn, did not believe in a "Supreme Synthesis," that is, in the ongoing creation of universal, dichotomy-transcending love, order, harmony, and unity among all human beings. Concepts like the punishment of sinners—their confinement in hell and purgatory—and a belief in the Antichrist, who, as part of divine providence, would devastate the world and torture Christians, assume a very different sense of divine order and intention for this world. A vision of a final humanistic victory of altruistic, unconditional love and universal sister/brotherhood is alien to Mechthild. Again, the problem of cultural differences and their implicit limiting influence on conceptualizing spiritual raw material comes into play here.

In contrast to Assagioli's depreciation of ecstatic states mentioned above, ecstasies are central elements of Mechthild's mysticism. They are the expression of as well as the channel for higher dimensions of consciousness (in her language, of God's loving presence). As alternatives to experiences of alienation, they are precursors of a more desirable state of being after death. Only ecstasies can give knowledge of the ground of being. Assagioli acknowledged that ecstasies occur during a spiritual psychosynthesis, but they are judged to be "pleasant side-effects" without significant impact; they are assigned little cognitive value. Classified as "awakening experi-

ences," they are not understood to induce a deep transformation of consciousness. Mechthild would agree with
Assagioli that at least some ecstatic states—those that
she dubbed "false ecstasies"—are spiritually worthless.
But as a religious specialist, Mechthild makes much
more systematic use of these states, and, unlike Assagioli, learns to differentiate types of ecstatic pleasure
and cognition.

Assagioli's goal of psychosynthesis, creativity, and al-
truism is identical with the "work" of the cosmos. Work
for the sake of her community, however, as important as
it is, does not appear as a goal in itself for Mechthild, but
as a means to an end. Even the writing of her books is
seen as an act of obedience to God, not to the ideal of
helping others (*The Flowing Light of the Godhead*, prologue). She never talks about compassion and help for
others as acts of *love*, be it *agape, caritas,* or *eros*. For her,
works of charity are acts of duty and means to an end (to
do the will of God and to be without sins). Her practice
of Minne is limited to the one-to-one exchange between
God and soul. The community of spiritual people in such
a context is that of a supportive "interest group," in
which each individual member seeks to establish personal ties to a loving Godhead.

From a psychosynthetic or even developmental perspective, one could speculate whether Mechthild might
have still been engaged in the process of a personal psychosynthesis. Most of her allegorical dialogues recount
the struggle of her inner forces for their unity and harmonization. Her capacity for love appears to be developed
only toward God, and the majority of her fellow human
beings are excluded. The center of her thoughts and actions is still perceived to be external (God) rather than
internal, something Assagioli describes in detail as a
characteristic of only partially realized Higher Selves.

Although Mechthild's teachings and Assagioli's tech-

niques of personal and spiritual psychosynthesis diverge,
they do converge in some points. Values such as self-dis-
cipline and the importance of the will in order to change
self-destructive and antisocial behavior and to control
undesirable character traits are common to both. A
thorough knowledge of oneself, though achieved with
different methods and in a different theoretical context, is
advocated by Mechthild as well: "I do not know anybody
who is so good that he does not need to prove his heart
incessantly and to realize what is in there and to criticize
his works frequently" (7, 2). Most interesting, however,
is the close resemblance of two of Assagioli's techniques
to Mechthild's major means of structuring and integrating her spiritual life: that is, mimesis and inner dialogue
with symbolic figures (allegories). Allegories like the
"Body," "Lady Understanding," and "Lady Minne" all
seem to play the role of Assagioli's "Inner Teacher."
Mechthild, however, uses these figures within a wider
range than psychosynthesis does. In the latter, these
imaginary teachers always represent a higher form of
consciousness (Assagioli 1981, 204), whereas for Mechthild they can also represent "inferior" but nonetheless
influential forces (as, for example, the body or the
senses). Those forces that in Assagioli's system are
deemed "lower"—(for example, split-off personality
traits, fears, conflicts, "ancestral or childish images that
obsess or silently dominate us" (21)—are granted an existence of their own as subpersonalities, or dominating
centers, but the therapeutic attitude toward these per-
sonae is one of mistrust and hostility. One may wonder
how well these subcenters can be "integrated" if the client is told that she is not fundamentally whole, but split,
tainted by parts of her personality that are a priori unac-
ceptable. Assagioli's language focuses on the patriarchal
language of alienation: "We are dominated by everything
with which our self becomes identified. We can dominate

and control everything from which we disidentify ourselves" (22). Mechthild's approach to the allegorical figures in her dialogues is much more tolerant: although the
body is an ambiguous force that separates her from full
fruition of the divine presence, she ultimately makes
peace with it as an unpleasant though necessary vehicle
for her life on earth. The same spirit of grudgingly
granted coexistence holds true for the manifestation of
her fears in the form of the devil; she can fall asleep while
the devil haunts her, and she can engage in wonderfully
witty rhetorical battles with him. In contemporary language, her psychological approach is one of letting be
and letting go rather than generating aggressive energy
to destroy and overcome what is perceived to be an
"enemy."

Mechthild's personal use of a mythical mimesis (the
passion of Christ) was possibly more intense and reen-
acted with greater existential involvement and radicality
than many of the mimetic exercises of Assagioli's clients.
Here we need to take into account the cultural climate of
the respective practitioners: for Mechthild, it was a much
more socially sanctioned enterprise to embark on an inner journey that employed well-established cultural paradigms than it is for a psychosynthesis client today to
explore her inner worlds through the fragments of long-
abandoned myths and highly subjective intuitions and
insights.

In conclusion, the similarities between Mechthild's
medieval mystical system and humanistic psychology
support the theses of researchers as different as Maslow
and Assagioli that transpersonal experiences extend beyond culture-bound theoretical superstructures. Ecstasies
did not stop occurring with the decline of Christian mysticism, and appear in the secularized society of the twen-

tieth century. Some religious structures as well survived the process of secularization. Although religious language is rejected in humanistic psychology, certain paradigms basic to the Jewish-Islamic-Christian mystical tradition re-emerge under a new name: the soul, a nonhuman source of being ("nature" or "cosmic energy"), and definitions of good and evil.

Mechthild's *soul*, a spiritual though passive part of a human being, is affected by the actions of an unnamed and unreflected upon "ego," which manifests itself through moral decisions; it is also intimately related to the body, which is of ambiguous status. Having a kind of Jungian "shadow" function, the body can either support or attack the well-being of the soul. For Maslow, the concept of *soul* is replaced by the notion of an "inner nature"—a potential that can either be stifled or manifested through self-actualization. Assagioli replaced the "soul" with four types of the unconscious and the superconscious, which can be explored by the conscious self or "I." Assagioli created a more complex and dynamic system of intrapsychic interaction, which is geared toward integration and harmonization of the different parts of the (un)conscious.

God for Mechthild is the experience of a complex divine Being, which is personal, consists of centers of action with diffuse boundaries (Father, Son, Holy Spirit, and divine love personified as Minne), and which relates to the human soul through the patterns of Minne as divine force. Maslow did not abandon the concept of a suprahuman cosmic being; he replaced "God" with a benevolent notion of "nature" but kept this concept generally undefined. Religiously speaking, Assagioli went further than Maslow. "God" is replaced by relatively neutral terms such as "cosmic energy" or "cosmic Being"; however, this energy possesses benevolent intention, moral judgment, and power.

Spirituality for Mechthild translates into the partially

individual, partially communal pursuit of the path of Minne; it also signifies the departure from a state of alienation or sin. Maslow replaced the spiritual journey with a striving for "naturalness," the optimal functioning of an individual or "self-actualization." Assagioli accepts the term *spirituality*. For him, it means the integration and harmonization of inner forces for the benefit of all human beings, a process that is part of a greater cosmic "Supreme Synthesis."

Evil plays a lesser role in Mechthild of Magdeburg's work than moral trespasses such as hypocrisy or slander. Personified as the devil, evil is understood as temptation, as alluring wrong choices. Evil is manifested in human action; it is unavoidable but not destroyable. Closest to evil in Maslow's system are *metapathologies;* defined as "illnesses," metapathologies are "natural" and can be overcome. Unfortunately, Maslow's premature death did not allow him to develop this notion further. For Assagioli, evil is simply the rejection of the goals of "Supreme Synthesis"; humans have full responsibility for evil. On the whole, however, this issue is not worked out in detail.

Values play a dominant role in all three models. For Mechthild, they are a necessary expression of spirituality; values are not a theoretical issue, but behavior- and group-oriented. They are not important in themselves (they are not secularized) but are expressions of the will of God. Values are the cornerstone of Maslow's humanistic psychology. "B-values" express self-actualization; they are mostly ego-centered and stress feelings of pleasure, enjoyment, and spontaneity. "D-values," on the other hand, express basic needs for healthy psychological functioning. Maslow did not show much concern for the social context of values; for him, values are aspects of being and nature. For Assagioli, values are based more on repression than expression; they are a necessary building block of cosmic synthesis.

Allegories and *symbols* have only limited significance for Maslow. For Assagioli, they are important representations of Higher Consciousness; they are intentionally used during therapy to open the client to "higher" dimensions of self and reality. Mechtild employed symbols to express and understand her mystical experiences and (for us) unusual aspects of psychic reality (devil, angels, Lady Minne, etc).

Ecstasies, finally, are preeminent expressions of "Beingness" for Maslow; they happen at random but carry significant cognitive value. For Assagioli, they are only symptoms of self-realization; they happen at random but have no greater meaning for the psychosynthetic process. Of all three authors, Mechthild has the most sophisticated model of ecstasies. They are defined as predominantly transformative states of union with a loving God; they are gifts given to the soul according to God's will and the soul's capacity to experience them. And finally, they are supreme carriers of ontological knowledge.

4

Healing and Intuition

Reflections of Mystical Consciousness in
Contemporary Psychotherapy

$\mathcal{T}$he two psychotherapeutic models I will discuss in this
chapter share with humanistic psychologies a concern for
values, inner growth and health. They are also distinctly
contemporary in their interpretation of holotropic states
as expresson of subjective rather than objective reality.
Unlike Maslow and Assagioli, however, their bias is toward psychological healing and the specific function of
the intuitive mode of awareness in that process. I chose
to include their theories in this section on ecstasies, because the intuitive mode as defined by Arthur Deikman,
a leading transpersonal psychotherapist, shares a number
of qualities with ecstasies. First, intuition, like ecstasy, assumes the existence of an Other with which the intuiting
subject merges in an act of emotionally open recognition.
Second, intuition favors the emergence of a set of values
that stress interdependence and open-endedness of inter-
actional processes. Third, the integration and practice of
the intuitive mode of awareness leads to the cultivation
of a qualitatively more complex and well-rounded self,
which, according to Mechthild of Magdeburg's teachings,
is also the result of the ecstatic path. For the sake of this
study, I approach intuition as the *cognitive* aspect of ecstatic states, which also include a strong emotionally and
energetically charged component.

Although the two models discussed below are the outcome of extensive psychotherapeutic praxis, the authors Arthur Deikman and Claudio Naranjo tend to write normatively rather than descriptively. Both models postulate the possibility of a synthesis of mysticism and psychotherapy. Arthur Deikman's contribution, summarized in his book *The Observing Self* (1982) is more theoretical (focusing on the nature of self and consciousness), whereas Claudio Naranjo is more concerned about techniques to induce a change of consciousness. Their work contributes additional terminology with which we can cross the cultural and historical divide between Mechthild's medieval and contemporary Western concepts of spiritual growth.

Intuitive Awareness and the Mystic Self

In *The Observing Self*, Arthur Deikman boldly defined mysticism as a "type of science," whose goal was to accumulate knowledge about the human mind. He postulated that mystics generally used religious terminology for "social necessity or convenience" only. Therefore, the theological aspects of mystical teachings do not have to be of particular heuristic value to contemporary research. But because any mystical system contains at its core a complex array of areligious knowlege about the nature of the self and human consciousness, modern psychology should take mystical knowledge seriously and integrate its discoveries in order to develop a more complete map of the self. Mysticism represents a "sophisticated appreciation of the relation between basic motives, cognition, and perception" (1982, 12).

Despite his insistence on the scientific character of mysticism, Deikman accepted the subjective, experiential nature of mystical "information-gathering" as a valid methodological tool. He compared mystical subjectivity to the notion espoused by quantum physics that perceiver and perceived form a dynamic, inseparable unit and as such render the notion of "objective" research absurd and impossible.

Rather than focusing specifically on ecstasy, Deikman explored two modes of consciousness which he called the *analytical/rational* and the *intuitive/mystical*. They roughly equal Grof's holotropic and hylotropic states of consciousness. Ideally, humans should be able to move freely back and forth between the two modes. Since Deikman is concerned about healing and mental well-being and critical of Western culture's overemphasis of rationality, he finds the cultivation of the intuitive mode of paramount therapeutic significance.

Arguing from a historical point of view, Deikman suggested that psychotherapeutic practice and theory should be seen in their propinquity to mysticism. Indeed, psychotherapy has been closer to mysticism than to traditional Western science (1982, 25). Healing, understood as a process involving both soul and body, was originally the task of the shaman, the medicine woman or medicine man, and the priest. Only slowly did the treatment of human ailments lose its holistic religious frame of reference. Finally, at the beginning of the twentieth century, psychotherapy was split into "organic" or physiologically oriented psychiatry and "psychogenic" therapy. This fissure, consolidating the already existing conceptual division between soul and body, became yet another marker of the end of a complementary bimodal soul-body consciousness in Western culture at large.

Using a model developed by Ellenberger (1974), which compares forms of "primitive" healing and modern scientifically oriented therapy, Deikman forcefully suggested that psychotherapy is closer to the dynamics of "primitive" healing than Western culture is willing to realize. It represents a form of "art" rather than "science." Intuition, subjectivity, empathy, and emotional communication play a greater role in healing than a merely rational observation devoid of emotion: "a therapist who responds to a patient with feelings of boredom, anger, sexual desire, enhanced self-esteem, or fear during a session can gain through those feelings information about the patient's activities and feelings, information that is usually more reliable than that conveyed by words or facial cues" (1982, 31).

The links between "primitive" healing practices and "sophisticated" mysticism are a reflection of their common methodology. Every mystic, Deikman claimed, achieves insight through intuition, a channel of knowing beyond rational processes (1982, 21), and the practice of virtues, which train the mind for higher forms of perception (89). Intuition is defined as a direct form of perception, in which the split between object and subject, characteristic of rational analysis, disappears: as in ecstasies, the perceiver becomes one with the perceived. Because intuition is also a receptive mode of consciousness, it is more capable of discerning subtle aspects of reality than rationality.

Deikman's emphasis on the differences between rationality and intuition as forms of knowing is, to a certain degree, reflected in the medieval distinction between *ratio* and *intellectio*.[1] The fusion between object and subject, which, according to Deikman, characterizes intuitive perception, was one of the major theological controversies in medieval mysticism—as fusion between Godhead and soul—and often led to charges of *autotheosis*. Deikman himself was aware of this issue; in contrasting Emile Durkheim's definition of religion with mysticism, he com-

1. See, for example, the texts *Benjamin Minor* and *Benjamin Major* of Richard of St. Victor (d. 1173).

mented, "followers of formal religions often try to affect the behavior of a god—propitiating, pleasing, and seeking aid. In contrast, the mystical tradition asserts the equation: I (Real Self) = God. While 'I am God' is the fundamental realization in mysticism, it is blasphemous in many religions" (1982, 3).

Despite his view of mysticism as a form of science, Deikman sharply distinguished his theoretical approach from most current psychological models, which he judged to be incomplete and limited in their understanding of the self. A full understanding of the self must acknowledge its transcendent and unlimited nature, which is at once individual and universal (1982, 65). To know the self, freedom from ego-centered interests and from a one-sided dependence on the analytical mode of consciousness is a *conditio sine qua non*. Referring to psychological theories on the interrelation between perception and motivation, Deikman claimed that the self as it is perceived in an analytical, nonintuitive frame of mind necessarily suffers from distortion, because perception itself is tainted by ego-centered motivation.[2] A change from ego-centered to altruistic motivation—facilitated by a shift from rational to intuitive awareness—can in turn change one's perception of reality and the interconnectedness of all life forms. Deikman concluded that historically only mystics were able to develop both types of awareness in harmony and consequently to realize a fully developed bimodal self.[3] It is of interest here that recent feminist research into modes of knowing make claims similar to Deikman's but add a gender-related dimension.

2. This statement of Deikman's is reminiscent of Maslow's values of self-actualizing persons, in particular transcendence of self, contributions to others, transcendence of selfish and merely personal motivations, and increased friendliness and kindness (1973b, 158).

3. For support of this argument in a case study of St. John of the Cross [1542–1591], see Sanderlin 1989.

In an extensive study of "women's ways of knowing," the researchers Mary Field Belenky, Blythe McVicker Clinchy, Nancy Rule Goldberger, and Jill Mattuck Tarule (1986), found it possible to formulate a concept of female "constructed knowledge" in which intuition and rationality complemented rather than excluded each other. With the exception of assigning gender labels to the two modes of awareness, Deikman thus presents a vision of the self that parallels closely feminist approaches such as the one by Belenky et al.[4]

Briefly, Deikman (1982, 72) defines the two modes as given in the table on p. 105.

In Deikman's view, the two modes of consciousness correspond not only to two sets of moral values but also to two types of self. The "object self" is the center that generates ordinary, limited, exclusively analytical perception. It evolves in early childhood when a child learns to act upon the environment. The object self operates in an "object mode," which "emphasizes the perception of differences and boundaries, the structuring of diffuse stimuli into manipulable entities" (Deikman 1982, 70). The perceptual order thus created is strictly functional, operating on the needs of self-preservation and acquisition (71). Although this mode is crucial for physical and psychological survival, it is not receptive to deeper currents of the psyche. In feminist theory, relying on this mode only is described as masculinist.

Deeper levels of the human psyche can be reached only by a complementary mode of consciousness, which

4. It should be noted that this simple bipolarity has been abandoned by more recent research on the brain, but it is easy to see how this model can lead to an interpretation of some aspects of mysticism as map of these two types of consciousness. A similar interpretation of ordinary consciousness has been formulated by Robert E. Ornstein (1972). See also Deikman 1973a.

Object Mode	Receptive Mode
Purpose	
To act on the environment	To receive the environment
Self	
Objectlike, localized, separate from others	Undifferentiated, unseparated from the world around it
Vantage point from which world is seen	Blurring of boundaries
Self-centered awareness	World-centered awareness
World	
Objects	Process
Absolute time	Relative Time
Consciousness	
Focal attention	Diffuse attention
Sharp perceptual boundaries	Blurred boundaries
Communication	
Verbal, unemotional	Music, art, poetry
Neurophysiology	
Left hemisphere dominance	Right hemisphere dominance
Increased beta waves	Decreased beta waves
Decreated alpha and theta waves	Increased alpha and theta waves

allows for the conceptual and perceptual fusion of self and environment. This type of fusion has traditionally been classified as nature mysticism (Happold 1981, 43). In this mode, logocentric analysis is replaced by intuition.

Awareness of the existence and respective relativity of these two complementary modes leads to the discovery and development of the authentic self, which Deikman called the *observing self*. Deikman described this self as a "transparent center." It is a detached inner faculty of awareness that is able to observe *all* emotional, rational, and intuitive functions of a human being. However, it cannot be observed or located, but only be known intuitively or "directly," that is, without a subject-object split. It is tautological to say that one can "become aware of awareness"; one can only experience awareness as awareness of *something*, because ultimately we *are* awareness. Besides this superior observing self, Deikman also distinguishes among three other motivational centers or subselves: the "conceptual self" (expressing thought), the "emotional self" (expressing feelings), and the "functional self" (the center for devising action). The function of all three subcenters is to maintain both a sense of reality as meaningful and a feeling of individuality (1982, 92).

In Deikman's view, psychotherapy and intuitive consciousness share a number of features with mysticism. How then is this seemingly secular model of the self mirrored in the religious cosmos of mysticism? In reflecting upon his own theory, Deikman admits that we cannot say exactly what the observing self is, but this fact in itself indicates "that the accepted psychological model of human beings is deficient in a basic way. It points to an unknown region whose exploration requires a radically different model of the self, one in which 'simple locality' is no longer assumed and the world view of mystics becomes a useful guide" (1982, 176). The goal of mystical techniques (different forms of meditation, instruction through teaching stories, etc.) is to teach how to perceive the "true self." According to Deikman, knowledge of the true self in turn necessarily leads to an understanding of the deep unity of all life-forms. Therefore, the recognition of the true self opens dimensions of ultimate (sacred) meaning and being. Knowledge of the self serves as "a bridge between the object world and the transcendent realm" (176). Although Deikman first rejected the value of religious content in mystical traditions, he now somewhat inconsistently acknowledges the objective nature of religious experience in the depth dimension of intuitive perception.

In contrast to the all-inclusive consciousness of the higher self, ordinary waking consciousness provides only a limited perspective of reality. Ordinary life, ruled by the dynamics of the "object self," is usually spent in a kind of trance or hypnotic state. With its limited functional perspective on reality, the mode of the object self engenders a number of behavior patterns similar to some characteristics of the hypnotic state. These patterns include restriction of awareness, fixed attention, and automatic responses to suggestions and commands (Deikman 1982, 120). All these symptoms share a loss of context and a limited frame of reference.

Deikman correlates the characteristics of the "object self" with his concept of object self formation in early childhood. The behavioral patterns implicit in the nature of the object self are first established in the interaction between powerful parents and a child who is relatively helpless but motivated to control her environment. If the child, when grown up, is not able to move beyond these early patterns and, implicitly, beyond the restraints of self-preserving and acquisitive motivation when such motivation is inappropriate, she will remain unaware of the greater possibilities of freedom and insight lying beyond the identification with the object self and the now mostly unconscious fantasy world of childhood experiences.

In order to break through the confinements of the limiting object mode, clients in a psychotherapeutic setting can be made aware of the restrictions of the object self and learn how to strengthen and to apply the mode of consciousness and perspective of the observing self. They thus gain a frame of reference that "extends beyond the dimensions with which we are familiar" (Deikman 1982, 129). This process resembles the act of awakening from a trance, but also the process of awareness/awakening training in mysticism. In Mechthild's context, this awakening is triggered by the *grus* that she received from childhood on, the "greeting" that propelled her into a new way of being and understanding.

Despite its proximity to mystical teachings, Deikman is careful to point out that his theory does not translate immediately into an advocacy of mystical techniques during psychotherapeutic sessions. The first and foremost task in integrating an expanded model of human consciousness should be to widen the conceptual framework of the *therapist*. Only as a result of the therapist's awareness training may she carefully assist the client to gain a deeper sense of self-awareness and liberation from harmful patterns of perception. In other publications Deikman refers to this therapeutic process as *deautomatization* (Deikman 1973a).

Deikman is careful in pointing out that mysticism should not be misunderstood as substitute for psychotherapy and vice versa. In his view, psychotherapy's task is primarily the treatment of psychopathology, unlike mysticism, whose task is to open up fully to new dimensions of awareness. Psychotherapy, when practiced in the expanded frame of reference Deikman suggests, should assist people only to reach the degree of inner centeredness and awareness that is the condition for a pursuit of the mystical path.

Deikman studied a wider variety of mystical systems than Maslow and Assagioli, in particular Sufism, Hasidic Judaism, Hinduism, and the mystical traditions in Greek philosophy. Christian mysticism plays a minor role in his writings. Nonetheless, he claimed that his statements about mysticism are universally valid. As the discussion

of Mechthild of Magdeburg's ecstasies in comparison to
Maslow and Assagioli's models has shown, such broad
generalizations can be problematic. Here I wish to focus
briefly on one issue: the evolution of a mystic, integrated
self.

Theism, the symbolic expression of a vision of existential and cosmic wholeness, integration, and the goal of
all human striving, Deikman replaced theism with the
concept of a relatively vaguely defined, nonreligious Self.
He replaced a complex theology of fullness of being, salvation, and a holy life with a theory of a psychophysiological type of awareness that procures a sense of
oneness with all life. What is a dialogical process between
human soul and God in monotheistic mystical teachings,
such as those of Sufism, Hasidism, or Christian mysticism, now becomes an inner movement from a lower,
fragmented self to a higher, integrated one. To a certain
degree, Deikman's model repeats Assagioli's hierarchical
structure of the qualitatively different types of the unconscious. A similar hierarchy appears in Jung's typology of
persona, shadow, and Self and in Maslow's distinction
between actualizing and nonactualizing sets of behavior
and values. Like their religious predecessors, these secular models do not abandon the concept of two qualitatively different dimensions of being (sacred and
profane), but simply introject into the human psyche
what has traditionally been an extraneous, objective, and
dialogical structure of reality. For Deikman and other humanist psychologists, the religious models ultimately operate with a defective definition of self imposed on them
by "social necessity or convenience." Reminiscent of Ludwig Feuerbach's theses on religion as projection, the
mystics' definition of the self is limited because it projects
human potential onto a divine being. Humanistic psychology returned the projected capacities for growth to

their proper owners and in turn destroyed a theocentric view of the world (see Fromm 1950). In contrast with Deikman's model, Mechthild of Magdeburg's mysticism serves as an important corrective to this reading. She shows that at least in regard to affective mysticism, the dialogical nature of ecstatic experiences of love destroys the hierarchical, oppressive, and therefore limiting aspects of a theocentric universe. God and human meet as equals, as in the following dialogue between God and soul. In the first part of the dialogue,

> God caresses the soul with six things:
> You are the pillow of my resting-place
> my bed of love
> my most secret repose
> my deepest desire
> my highest splendor.
> You are the lust of my divinity
> the solace of my humanity
> a [cooling] creek to my heat.
>
> (1, 19)

The soul in turn praises God with six things:

> You are my mirror mountain
> a feast for the eyes
> a loss of my self
> a storm of my heart
> a fall and decline of my powers
> my highest certainty.
>
> (1, 20)

The soul clearly experiences a conceptual shift, a disclosure of a higher state of being as part of the divine self (God's deepest desire, highest splendor). The encounter described above is empowering in the humanist sense, but with one difference. The higher self is constructed in communion with an Other, not in opposition to it. As such it sharply contrasts the model of the isolated heroic self of patriarchy that is coiled inward and mostly incapable of peaceful and constructive interaction with an other. Although the seed of this postpatriarchal vision is inherent in Deikman's appraisal of an intuitive grasp of the world as basically unified, Deikman has not fully developed its implications for a higher self in relation with others. Mechthild's medieval universe—in its textual as well as material manifestions—is populated if not crowded with creatures natural and supernatural who interact, confront, caress, provoke, witness. The contemporary universe of theories on ecstatic states and intuition is in comparison sterile, sanitized, bleak with isolation. This contrast is thought-provoking; the answer to the question of vision of the self is more "humanist," I think, points in the direction of Mechthild.

One last theme in Deikman's theory deserves to be mentioned. He indirectly offers an interesting commentary on Mechthild's nonanalytical, poetic style. To some extent, her dialogues and narratives resemble the teaching stories of Sufism and Hasidic Judaism, which Deikman discusses extensively in his chapters on the possibilities of applying mystical techniques in psychotherapy. He points out the subliminal influence of teaching stories, whose often paradoxical and humorous imagery and messages can bypass ordinary consciousness and thus affect the deeper levels of intuitive understanding and perception. (Another religious example of this technique is the use of a Koan in Zen Buddhism.)

Because of their poetic and narrative character, Mechthild's dialogues, descriptions, stories, and images, like Sufi stories, defy rational, logical concreteness but appeal directly to the emotional, receptive, intuitive dimension of the mind. As such, the effect of her teachings is psychologically more powerful than it may appear on first sight, if her reader becomes immersed in the text. Her advice to read *The Flowing Light of the Godhead* nine times, for example, can be interpreted as a reinforcement of the subliminal effects of her poetry: that is, to submerge one-self in its rhythm and imagery, to stop the ordinary mode of extraverted, action-oriented thinking and to enter the realm of the receptive, intuitive mode. In the light of this psychological interpretation of her instruction and dic-tion, we recognize a greater continuity between Mechthild's ecstasies and the experiences she promised to her readers: both appear as phenomena on the continuum of the receptive mode.

A Threefold Typology of Awareness Training: Concentration, Negation, Self-Surrender

In the first part of a book coauthored with Robert Orn-stein, Claudio Naranjo, a well-known research psychia-trist at the University of California at Berkeley, discussed the practical aspects of mysticism and their relationship to psychotherapy (Naranjo and Ornstein 1977). Naranjo, like Deikman, regarded psychotherapy as a form of art, even a type of mysticism. According to him, some of its features can be traced back to "primitive" mysticism (shamanism, magic). Unlike Deikman, however, Naranjo assumed that all major insights and descriptions of "in-ner" and "outer" reality in mysticism are at their core identical, because they point to the same ultimate reality. The core teachings of Christian mysticism are not differ-ent from those of Sufism or Eastern mystical schools. As he puts it, "everything is the same, and everything is dif-ferent. Perhaps this last statement sums up the only im-portant thing I have to say" (1977, 132).

The common practical denominator of all mystical systems is meditation, which Naranjo classifies in a bril-

liant simplification into three types: concentration, negation, and self-surrender. All three function as "awareness
training." Naranjo then goes on to argue that despite
their seeming differences, all three paths lead to the same
goal. Since his thesis is illustrated by references to religious texts from the Hindu, Buddhist, Islamic, and Christian traditions, his theory is more accessible to a scholar
of religion than most of the writings of previously discussed theorists.

Naranjo, like Deikman, assumes that all forms of
mysticism share a focus on the dynamics of human consciousness and the goal to refine and improve awareness
of the self. This mental process is accompanied by intentional changes of behavior. Mysticism is seen primarily as
a process that synchronizes body and mind. Naranjo
thus emphasizes the practical aspect of mysticism, the direct manipulation of behavior in order to influence consciousness. In his words, mysticism fosters the "de-
structuring [of] individual behavior in order to facilitate
the emergence of inner structure" (1977, 117), a trait that
it shares with psychotherapy.

Like Deikman, Naranjo is interested in the two fundamental modes of consciousness rather than in the
broader spectrum of states of consciousness. What he
calls "ordinary" limiting waking awareness is similar to
Deikman's analytical/rational mode; meditative awareness, approximating Deikman's intuitive mode, is seen as
receptive, unhampered by preconception and prejudice,
and open to the deeper levels of reality which are closed
to ordinary perception. Naranjo reasons that because
deeper truths about reality and the self can be discovered
only in a meditative frame of mind, mystics were drawn
to study the differences and qualities of the two types of
consciousness and ways to cultivate "higher," nonordinary consciousness.

As mentioned above, the three meditative techniques

of concentration, negation, and self-surrender lead to the same goal, although their basic assumptions about the relation between ordinary and meditative consciousness appear to be different at first glance. Concentrative or absorptive meditation employs an archetypal symbol as point of focus (e.g., the five-pointed star, the cross, the circle of yin and yang, the mandala). Its aim is the subject's absorption into the objective, sacred reality represented by the symbol; the goal is experienced as ego-dissolution and union with the divine. In relation to the self, such union means the discovery of one's center and the identification with the cosmic ground of one's being (Naranjo and Ornstein 1977, 23). "To the extent that we are 'ourselves', we are also part of the cosmos, a tide in the ocean of life, a chain in the network of processes that do not either begin or end within the enclosure of our skins" (34). Meditation aids in facilitating this insight, and thus is always a form of worship (36). Seen in this theoretical context, *nirvana, fana-f'illah*, and a Christian experience of union with God are identical.

The "negative way" teaches detachment from and elimination of all behavioral habits, routines, and rigidly held contents of consciousness. These behaviorally and conceptually inflexible patterns are not reality, but only the results of biased filtering mechanisms of the ego during states of "ordinary" awareness. Although it is not their stated purpose, the other two types of meditation reach the same goal as that of negation, that is, an emptying of the mind of compulsive preoccupations with images and thoughts. During the process of rejecting the falsely constructed world of objects and thoughts, a state of inner freedom and equanimity is established. For an Eastern example of the "negative way," Naranjo describes the rules of the *Patanjali sutras*, which promote purification (eliminating all distracting objects and thoughts), emotional detachment, and asceticism. As

Western models, Naranjo cites Christian practices of an ascetic renunciation of the world. His examples include the writings of Pseudo-Dionysius (end of 5th, beginning of 6th c.), Meister Eckhart (ca. 1260–1328), Richard of St. Victor (d. 1173), St. John of the Cross (1542–1591), the Desert Fathers, and the Alexandrian Gnostics. The purpose of negation resembles somewhat Deikman's notion of deautomatization. In Naranjo's terms, it is a "state in which 'consciousness abides in itself' and is experienced as independent from all psychophysiological mechanisms" (1977, 78).

The key characteristic of self-surrender, or the "expressive way," is its emphasis on the spontaneous flow of self-expression, coupled with a simultaneously practiced detached observation of this unfolding. The practitioner trusts that the blocking mechanisms of ordinary consciousness will be overcome if mind and body are allowed to express themselves freely. The key terms in this method are *surrender* and *self-expression*. During this type of meditative practice, the conscious ego is reduced to the status of a mere observer, a "non-intruding witness of nature" (1977, 115), a concept reminiscent of Deikman's definition of the "observing self." Visual representations are expected to emerge freely from the realm of archetypes. The free-association technique of psychoanalysis, artistic creation, and the vision quest of the Great Plains Indians are interpreted as examples of opening up to the visual dimension through the act of "letting go." Psychedelic drugs like peyote or LSD, the *latihan* sessions of Sufism, or Za-Zen are used in other examples of means to achieve liberation through a surrender to and trust in the natural emergence of the "deeper" structures of awareness. A comparable model in Christianity is affective mysticism, in which mystics cultivate emotional expressions of love. As I have indicated in the analysis of Mechthild's ecstasies, spiritual focus on Minne can generate an impressive spectrum of feelings reaching from utter desolation to highest bliss. All emotions are carefully observed, analyzed, and cultivated as to their usefulness in achieving union with the divine and transformed self.

As Naranjo saw it, almost all schools of Christian mysticism are examples of the model of concentrative meditation. The exclusive focus on God, the desire for the experience of union with God, and a movement away from the interests of the ego (what Naranjo called "outer-directedness"), are defined as the most prominent Christian features of concentrative exercises. Although many examples can be found that support Naranjo's thesis, characteristics of the other two types of meditative practice can be documented within Christianity as well. As specific manifestations of the expressive way, one may point to the poetic and prophetic creativity of mystics, which went beyond merely reduplicating Christian dogma, to the already mentioned emotionality of affective mysticism, or to a mystic's sense of freedom from and critique of established behavior norms (see, for example, the biography of St. Francis of Assisi or St. Elisabeth of Thuringia). The traditional Christian categories of apophatic (moving beyond language, concepts, physical phenomena) and cataphatic (affirming the world and our descriptions of it as valid depositories of knowledge of the divine) mysticism cover some aspects of Naranjo's threefold model, yet without distinguishing between the cataphatic "subcategories" of concentration and expression.

Although Naranjo includes theistic mystical traditions, Buddhist perspectives provide most of his vocabulary and categories for interreligious comparison—influencing, for example, his judgment that statements about divine being have only metaphorical value, his opinion on the relativity of ordinary perception, and his focus on consciousness in its different manifestations. Christian mysticism, interpreted exclusively through these categories, is in danger of being reduced to a technique for changing subjective consciousness. As mentioned earlier, for a Christian mystic, the manipulation of consciousness in Naranjo's sense is generally a goal secondary to her attempt to come closer to God existentially and to do God's will in the human community.

Mechthild's text supports this rather broad definition of Christian mysticism. Mechthild certainly was aware that different states of consciousness would push her beyond the noetic confinements of her "earth-bound" knowledge, but the achievement of such states was understood as processes that would transform not just her consciousness, but her total self and her role in her community. It is the total self in the totality of its social, psychological, and mystical contexts that God addresses in book 1, chapter 36:

> You shall be adorned with the malice of your enemies
> You shall be ennobled with the virtues of your heart
> You shall be crowned with your good works
> You shall be exalted with the love [that exists] between
>   the two of us
> You shall be sanctified with my lustful wonder.

Moreover, ecstatic states were judged to be beyond her conscious control. No matter whether her experiences of altered states were positive (ecstasies) or negative (desolation experiences), they were seen as controlled by God, given as either gifts of love (union ecstasies) or gifts of mercy (withdrawal of his potent "energy," his "light," in order to keep her alive). Only preparatory stages could be influenced by her (for example, through virtuous behavior, prayer, or attending mass).

In the context of this study, Naranjo's model is most useful for his description of the *process* itself, which leads to new insights about the nature of self, reality, and consciousness. Interpreted with the assistance of Naranjo's categories, Mechthild's meditative practices appear less as random idiosyncratic phenomena than as a variation of globally shared human patterns of consciousness transformation. In *The Flowing Light of the Godhead*, elements of the "expressive way," the "concentrative way," and the "negative way" can easily be identified. Ascetic practices, representations of the "negative way," appear to be taken for granted but play only a minor role in Mechthild's mystical teachings. Although she saw ascetic exercises as tools to control the will of the body, she established no causal connection between castigating her body and experiencing ecstasies. According to Mechthild, her ascetic "training" lasted for twenty years and resulted in tiredness and illness (4, 2); courting God, cultivating good intentions, and acting ethically were better "tools" for transformation. Deepening her love of God, practicing compassion, and strengthening her will could be interpreted as elements of concentrative exercises, because they help her shed all concerns about "worldly" preoccupations in order to become closer to God. But even so, Mechthild of Magdeburg never ceased emphasizing her own impotence and her dependence upon God in regard to the process of transformation: "Dear people, how could I have caused what is happening to me now and has happened so often in the past? In humble simplicity and in solitary poverty and in oppressing disgrace God has shown me his miracles" (4, 2). It is obvious that such a stated distrust in human power, whose usefulness is questioned from the onset, limits the efficacy of any spiritual technique. Mechthild would agree with Naranjo (and Deikman), however, that the insights that are gained from nonordinary types of awareness can cause change and induce growth. As a result of God's transformative, loving influence, the soul through ecstasy becomes aware of the true nature of God. The recognition of her innate goodness and nobility precedes her union with God and is a necessary precondition for it. Mechthild scorned the "blind saints" who practiced Minne but did not understand its true meaning (1, 2).

Both Deikman and Naranjo believe that intentionally induced changes in patterns of consciousness have adaptive, psychotherapeutic value. Such changes can lead to psychic integration, expansion of awareness, and freedom from mental constructs that govern habitual perception. Deikman moved toward a definition of psychic integration based on a bimodal view of self and consciousness. Naranjo offered a theory on the different ways in which spiritual practitioners or clients in a psychotherapeutic setting could achieve inner freedom, self-respect, and creativity. Although the ideas of Deikman and Naranjo shed light on Mechthild's teachings, there are distinct differences as well—most importantly, in regard to a dialogical understanding of reality and community in the formation of the integrated self. From Mechthild's perspective, techniques alone are not sufficient tools for healing.

5

Visionary Experiences

Holotropic States and the Construction of Knowledge

> Now beauty, as we said, shone bright amidst
> these visions, and in this world below we appre-
> hend it through the clearest of our senses, clear and
> resplendent. For sight is the clearest mode of per-
> ception vouchsafed to us through the body. (Plato,
> *Phaedrus*, 250d)

*M*echthild interpreted ecstasies as existentially and
conceptually transformative events; for her, ecstatic states
revolve around a relationship between the self and divine
reality that is explored through emotions and intense experiences of union. Visions, on the other hand, are the
medium in which the relationship between a human being and the divine is translated back into the fabric of
"ordinary" life.[1]

Historically, visionary experiences in the West were
first conceptualized as journeys into the world of the
dead. Since the twelfth and thirteenth century, encounters with Christ, the Virgin Mary, and saints began to
predominate. These encounters often carried reformatory
messages critical of society and the Church (Dinzelbacher
1989a, 31). At their most daring, visions were utopian; at
their most ordinary, corrective and prescriptive. They

---

1. For organic factors involved in the visionary event, see Meissner 1992, 318–28.

point out what could and what should be. In *The Flowing Light of the Godhead*, visionary accounts reflect concerns of Mechthild's community—the loss of family members, personal guilt, religious issues, injustice, war—and offer solutions. Within the context of her community, visions heal, create alternatives, resolve contradictions. Especially for medieval religious women, the visionary mode functioned as an alternative, publicly acknowledged way to construct meaning and to affect the community at large. In her seminal work on medieval women visionaries, Elizabeth Petroff developed a gynocentric model of visions, noting accurately that in the Middle Ages "Visions led women to the acquisition of power in the world while affirming their knowledge of themselves as women. Visions were a socially sanctioned activity that freed a woman from conventional female roles by identifying her as a genuine religious figure" (1986, 6).

In her typology of women's visions, Petroff does not distinguish clearly between ecstasies and visions.[2] What she calls participatory, unitive/erotic, and devotional visions may frequently be ecstatic experiences rather than symbolically coded cognitive processes. On the other hand, this lack of differentiation indicates quite correctly that the distinction between these two types of altered states can often merge in mystical experience. Hadewijch's visions are a good example of the fusion and interdependence of ecstasies and visions. In Mechthild of Magdeburg's text, however, we find so many accounts of nonecstatic mystical auditory and visual experiences that

2. Petroff (1986) describes several stages of visionary experiences: purgative, psychic, doctrinal, devotional, participatory, unitive/erotic, and cosmic. Ernst Benz, in his *Magnum opus Die Vision* (1969), distinguishes between five types of visions; his concept is a mix of formal and functional visionary characteristics, which make it difficult to use for a comprehensive classification. Benz differentiates between light, dream, prophetic, reaffirmative, and teaching visions.

a differentiation between ecstasies and visions as distinct mystical events should be made.

Visions reveal intriguing aspects of Mechthild's role as spiritual teacher. Mechthild's ecstasies, presented as exemplary transformative processes, were intended to be reexperienced by her audience, but visions are her exclusive and unique property. In most of the cases, her visions have merely cognitive value for her readers: that is, they will not be able to reexperience them like an ecstasy.[3]

How did Mechthild's visions work for her and her audience? As Margaret Miles has shown so persuasively in her study of visions in fourteenth-century Italy, for the ordinary medieval viewer, images in general carried a much greater impact and were invested with stronger emotional energy than they do in contemporary culture (Miles, 1985; Duffy 1992; Ziegler 1993). The process of mystical en-visioning, we might conjecture, was valued not only because of the high esteem for any image but also because it ignited an active process of re-creation and exploration on the part of the experiencing subject. (Contemporary "visual relaxation" techniques probably come closest to a rediscovery of the medieval approach to religious images.) Looking at a painting or sculpture and experiencing visions bear a remarkable resemblance to each other in Mechthild's descriptions. The visionary core images are often static *tableaux vivants* that patiently expose themselves to her gaze and in turn to the minds of her audience.

Perhaps more so than ecstasies, visions are embedded in a socioimaginistic fabric that we can reconstruct only with some difficulty. The visionary message appears to be a response to the day-to-day lives of medieval people, who lived in a culture that was predominantly oral, not

3. For an exception to this rule see, for example, the vision in 2, 21.

literary. The language Mechthild used to describe ecstasies, on the other hand, encoded to a large degree in the specialized vocabulary of "high culture," can be more easily related to the literary traditions of her time. For a contemporary reader, Mechthild's accounts of visions appear as fragments torn from a larger popular spiritual context that is more difficult to reconstruct than the relatively smoothly correlated segments of the more accessible mysticotheological discourse of her times. In the textual order of *The Flowing Light of the Godhead*, no explanatory text precedes or follows visions: they are interspersed narrative islands in the larger poetic flow of her writings. Only brief introductions to the visions themselves link Mechthild as recipient of visionary information to a certain religiously marked time or state of mind. Typical for Mechthild (as for other visionaries) are brief opening sentences such as "In one night I happened to be in prayer during the first phase of sleep . . ." (4, 2).

Because of their immediate relevance to the life of her community, the images of Mechthild's visions are more diverse and often more concrete than those used to describe her ecstasies. The structure of Mechthild's visionary accounts is remarkably uniform, usually consisting of three parts. After (1) an introduction explaining how and/ or why Mechthild received the vision *(authentification)*, (2) one or more core image(s) *(visual and/or auditory message)* are spun into (3) explanatory dialogues, comments, and remarks that are often presented as part of the vision itself *(verbal explanation)*.

Mechthild's visions fall into three major categories that often overlap: didactic, doctrinal, and cosmic. We find a few psychic visions (displaying clairvoyance or cardiognosis [the reading of hearts], for example), which give information about the spiritual state of Mechthild's contemporaries and often contain premonitions about deaths and births. Compared to other types, however, they are rare. The oldest documented Western type of visions, discovering the whereabouts of souls after death, are somewhat more frequent.

Mechthild's numerous *doctrinal* and *cosmic* visions are generally utopian in character. According to Petroff's definition, doctrinal visions resolve spiritual dilemmas, appear in the form of parables, and are pedagogical in intent (Petroff 1986, 9). Because of their theological coloring they can be part of an ongoing discussion between a mystic and her confessor. They may address a larger community, if, as in the case of Mechthild, the mystic is recognized as authority beyond the confines of a monastic community. In a gynocentric visionary universe, a cosmic vision "presents the feminine as the operative principle in the cosmos" (Petroff, 1986, 19; see also Newman, 1990). This definition needs to be modified in light of Mechthild's writings; for her, the feminine is certainly not the central operative principle of the universe, but it is nonetheless a highly visible and potent symbol as Virgin Mary, soul-bride, and Minne.

Despite their thematic variety, the function of all of Mechthild's visions is *didactic*. Didactic visions have been labeled "the least attractive" of all visions, because they lack dramatic effects and aesthetic stimuli (Benz 1969, 150–63, my trans.). Aesthetic stimuli are certainly plentiful in Mechthild's visions, but they are gentle and invite a long, quiet gaze rather than arrest eyes in awe and terror. A didactic vision aims at the communication of religious insights and ethical guidelines. Generally, visual imagery is curtailed in favor of auditive elements. The former serves merely as framework for the statements of a supernatural or human teacher. Typical of didactic visions is the appearance of a human mediator who transfers the message from the spiritual to the earthly realm. The interpretation can be part of the vision or added to it either before or after the showing of visual symbols. As examples of a teaching vision, Benz mentions such diverse texts as the letters to the angels of the seven communities in the Apocalypse, Hildegard of Bingen's and Julian of Norwich's works, and a number of Emmanuel Swedenborg's (1688–1772) visions. For Benz, the didactic vision is placed at the end of the visionary spectrum because it begins to dissolve what he regards as the genuine features of a vision, that is, its dramatic and aesthetic constituents. In terms of style, traditional forms of instructive speech supersede symbol and allegory: exegesis, sermon, and apologetics can easily be identified. Perhaps because these stylistic formats have been a male prerogative, they are almost nonexistent in Mechthild's text.

In the following pages, I will present a detailed analysis of the six visions in book 2 to introduce the reader to the richness and complexity of this mode of consciousness in Mechthild's work. Then, in the next chapter, I will discuss contemporary theories that help to elucidate the processes occuring during the visionary experience.

Visions in Book 2

The second book introduces the visionary genre in its full thematic richness and as such carries paradigmatic value for the rest of Mechthild's work. It varies both in size and content from the first book, which supplied most of the ecstatic accounts described at the beginning of my study, although some familiar forms and themes recur. Ecstasies are mentioned seven times, but only twice are they part of a more elaborated set of teachings. Book 2 comprises twenty-six chapters of varying length—from fourteen up to about thirteen hundred words—and prose outweighs poetry. Although it is difficult to detect a common theme running through all parts, the dominance of a narrative style suggests the author's mood here is more reflective and discursive than emotionally expressive and evocative.

Visions and Teaching Authority

Direct remarks about Mechthild's self-understanding as a writer are sparse throughout the second book; only at the end do we find a chapter dedicated to "this book and its writer." This final chapter contains a dialogue between God and the soul, a prayer for the protection of the book and the book's copiers, and a commentary addressed to her friends. In the dialogue Mechthild compares herself to a "learned spiritual man," but she uses this comparison only to highlight the gap between her real social status as "uneducated" woman and what her society accepts as theologically and spiritually respectable. The self-deprecating remark that her work should have been written by a male scholar in order to find a well-disposed audience tells us indirectly that, consciously or not, Mechthild is indeed usurping a place and status reserved for a sex and class of people to which she did not belong (see Poor 1994).

> Oh Lord, if I were a learned religious man, and you had worked this rare, great miracle through him, you would have received eternal glorification. How can one believe that you built a golden house in a filthy slough and live in it with your mother and all creatures? . . . Lord, earthly wisdom cannot find you there (2, 26).

Mechthild's social betwixt-and-between status is eased on a spiritual level. What others label as inappropriate usurpation can also be interpreted as freedom: "Free Minne must always remain the highest goal for a human being" (2, 26). In Middle High German, the adjec-

tive *vri* vacillates between the description of a social status, being free-born, and the psychological condition of
possessing an open and unencumbered spirit, free of
concern. It can also refer to not being bound, captured,
or in chains.[4] In a religious context, the term has a long
tradition (see Schweitzer 1981, pt. 2). Another Beguine,
Marguerite Porète (d. 1310), made the notion of a freed
soul one of the cornerstones of her theology (Schweitzer
1981, 52; Ruh 1984, 226). For Marguerite Porète, the dynamic of freedom allows one to break through earthly,
limited reality into the transcendence of the divine to
reach one's true destiny. Somewhat related to Marguerite
Porète's teachings is Mechthild's view of freedom as part
of the *imago dei* character of the human soul, which represents the ground of her dignity: "Lady Understanding, I
was born noble and free," declares the soul (2, 19). The
radicality and latent feminism of this insight is, however,
curtailed by the ambivalence Mechthild inherits from the
ascetic tradition. The potential of liberation is stymied by
rejection of the body. The oppression by others appears
to be (at least partially) introjected and experienced as oppression by her "earthly" self. Instead of asking to be de-
livered from the pain inflicted by others, Mechthild asks
to be saved from her time-and-place–bound bodily self:
"But if you will it, Lord, I will be freed of myself" (1, 46).

Freedom, the realization of her innate dignity, *without*
struggle thus can be experienced only momentarily dur-

4. In summary, "free" (*vri*) is used in a number of ways in book 2:
first, to denote the absence of suffering in highly developed *Minne*
("free love lives without pain of the heart" 2, 11); second, to underline
the high ontological status of the soul ("Lady Understanding, I [i.e.,
the soul] was born noble and free" 2, 11); third, to denote a higher
state of spirituality (Lady Minne admonishes the soul, "If you want to
dwell with him in noble freedom, you have to move out of the lodg-
ings of bad habit" 2, 23); and fourth, to depict the true nature of *Minne*
("because free *Minne* must remain the highest part of a human
being").

ing the ecstatic meetings with a liberating God. The genius of Mechthild's spirituality is that she does not stay within the confinements of such "secrecy." To experience freedom *with* struggle is to tell the secret of her spiritual knowledge, even if ascetic denial and liberating self-affirmation clash in a paradox. Mechthild is the revealer of God's mysteries; freedom manifests itself when she teaches and communicates. Thus God can tell her, "now see in all these words / how praiseworthy they describe my secrets / and do not have doubts about yourself" (2, 26).

The Secret Message

Reading the book nine times was the device advocated in book 1, opened the text to a mystical dimension. In book 2, Mechthild uses yet another tool. The book's print, its parchment, and the process of reading represent—*pars pro toto*—the Trinity much as relics contain and transmit the power of saints. The parchment is a likeness of God's humanity, the letters show forth his divinity, and the sound of the words re-present the Holy Spirit. Mechthild uses the verb *bezeichenen*, which Lexer (1872) translates into modern German as "bildlich vorstellen, mit einem Zeichen ausdrücken; bedeuten, vorbedeuten" ("express through an image, to communicate with a sign; to mean, to prefigure"). The relationship between symbolized and symbol here is comparable to the inspirational relationship between an object of devotional art and its devotee.

Such fusion of message and sender has been called a "mysticism of the book."[5] Reading and writing become

5. See Schweitzer, 1981, 101; the quotation is from Walter Muschg (1935, 236). According to the material Manfred Günter Scholz collected, it was a common formula to write that the words themselves

magical acts. As magical acts, they ward off those who can hurt Mechthild. It is in such a mystical/magical context that she receives and disseminates her visions.

Taken as a whole, the visions cover topics that move from the cosmic (2, 3) to the psychological and moral (2, 21), from the theme of the redemption of creation to the beatification of a single human being. The split between Mechthild's narrative and experiential self is not as distinct as in the ecstasies. Sometimes Mechthild is even unsure which part of her is involved in the event and which is not. She mentions, for example, that "During my prayer, it happened to me in such a way that I do not know whether the kingdom of heaven bowed down to me or whether I was pulled into the pleasurable house of God" (2, 20). It is remarkable that Mechthild had little inclination to explain the inner workings of the visionary experience and was content to note that she simply did not know. From this contrast with her elaborate and frequent attempts to describe and analyze ecstasies, we might conclude that visions were a long-standing, accepted, and therefore comparatively unproblematic tradition at Mechthild's time, while ecstasies were still approached as rather unusual and therefore in need of explanation.

Crossbow and Rose Petals. In book 2, chapter 3 is the first vision in a series of four that appear to be loosely related to each other. They are arranged in almost successive order (chapters 3, 4, 7, and 8; chapters 5 and 6 are a comparatively brief "song" and "returned song" by God and soul, a so-called *Wechselgesang*). All deal with an aspect of Christian symbolism (paradise, mass,

---

"talk" or "tell." Scholz uses this metaphor to suggest that loud reading was not as frequent as commonly assumed (1980, 125–35).

the blood of Christ, and purgatory), whereas the remaining two visions later on in the book (chapters 20 and 21) exclude any theological issue and discuss strictly ethical questions.

The first (2, 3) has a beginning typical of a didactic vision; it combines a verbal and a visual element, which together set the tone for instruction: "God's great tongue told me many vigorous words which I received with the weak ears of my lowliness / and the most shining light opened to the eyes of my soul."[6] The vision itself is divided into four parts. Mechthild's commentary on the core imagery serves as an introduction and sets the tone for what is to come. What she has seen is "unspeakable order," "incomprehensible wonder," "unmitigated joy in union," and "living love in eternity." The remaining three sections describe the Trinity, Mary, and Christ, respectively, as they relate to human beings.

In the second part, Mechthild depicts how divine love frees human souls. Four beams from God's crossbow, each symbolizing an aspect of the Godhead (light, friendship, joyful "energy," breath), are aimed at human beings and fill them with Minne. Souls are set free as sparks disperse from a burning log: with great ease, they glide through the air "wherever they want." The third

6. Benz dedicates a full chapter to the forms of "heavenly light" in mystical events. Biblical sources include, for example, 1 Timothy 6:16 ("He is King of kings and Lord of lords; he alone possesses immortality, dwelling in unapproachable light), Matthew 17: 1, 2 ("Six days later Jesus . . . led them up a high mountian where they were alone; and in their presence he was transfigured; his face shone like the sun, and his clothes became white as the light"), Paul's conversion experience in Acts 9: 3 ("While he was still on the road and nearing Damascus, suddenly a light flashed from the sky all around him"), or Psalm 119: 105 ("Thy word is a lamp to guide my feet and a light on my path"). For a discussion of the neoplatonic tradition of light as metaphysical metaphor, especially in the work of Nicholas of Cusa, see Fuehrer, 1986.

pattern of imagery in this section connects the metaphorically coded movement of souls: the tension of directed motion (pointed beam from crossbow) and softly
exploding diversion (freed souls that fly through the air)
are harmonized in the vision of a harp. What first appears as arrow unleashing emprisoned energies reveals
itself at the end as divine orchestration. The Trinity
plucks the (human) strings of a harp, which in turn reso-
nate with divine sound (See also Schmidt 1990, 80–83).

The third and fourth parts of the vision unfold like
two wings of an altarpiece. To the left of God the Father
stands Mary, her breasts dripping milk. On the right,
Jesus Christ parallels Mary in gesture and position: just
as milk flows from her breasts, so blood trickles from his
open wounds.[7] Motion as trajectory of divine energy was
the axis around which the second part of this vision re-
volved; time takes its place in the third and fourth sections. At the Last Judgment, Mechthild writes, the bodies
of Mary and Christ will be transformed: Mary's body will
be beatified; Christ's wounds will stop bleeding. This image can be traced to Origen (185/6–254) and was still used
by St. Bernard of Clairvaux (1090–1153). According to
Origen, Christ, Mary, and the blessed remain in a condition of waiting and imperfection until the Day of Judgment (Mechthild of Magdeburg 1956, 426). In Mechthild's
vision, Christ's bleeding flesh will turn into scars resembling rose petals. Mary's body will be transfigured by the
light of the soul: "Then the uncreated God / will recreate
all his creations / and make them so very new that they
never can age again." All parts of this vision share one
motif, that of eschatological transformation. The underlying theme of all transformation is the tension between
the body as vulnerable target—exposed to pain (Christ's

7. For the parallelism of these medieval images, see Bynum 1987,
277–94.

wounds), immobile (human bodies that cannot yet fly), and aging—and the body transformed—healed (rose petals instead of wounds), at ease and flexible (swiftly flying), redeemed in its sensuality (Mary's swelling breasts), and eternally young (a gift granted after the Day of Judgment). Three times in this short text, body and soul are described as being in harmony. Luminescent human beings "fly, wherever they want to with body and with soul." The force of gravitation and its symbolic value are abandoned, but without a destruction of the nature of either body or soul: "and they remain unmixed in their different functioning." Mary is first perceived "with body and soul / as she will always remain / yet now without the great beauty / which the father will give . . . at the Last Judgment." In none of the images does Mechthild reject the aesthetic ideals of courtly love. Like courtly love, her religiosity is at its core sensual and physical. In book 1, chapter 44, Mechthild explicitly rejects the nonerotic asceticism represented by Mary Magdalene ("Be silent [about her]. . . . You all do not know what I mean"), the chastity of virgins ("this is not the highest thing I have"), or the childlike love represented by Jesus as infant. She sees herself as "full-grown bride," sensual, sexual, with adult responsibilities.

On one level, then, Mary represents the potentials of this bride: beauty, youth, physicality and abundant fertility. It is interesting, though, that the act of impregnation itself is not an issue; virginal motherhood in this context affirms female independence and procreational power, not patriarchal dependence (see Beer 1992). Note that Mary's counterpart in the vision is the wounded godcompanion; the religious archetype of the goddess and her consort shimmers through the layers of Christian imagination.

Mechthild focuses on the motif of eschatological reconciliation between body and soul a second time in book

2. In a dialogue between Minne and the soul, the rebellious soul first rejects with refreshing honesty all invitations to follow the tedious ascetic path suggested by Minne. She "rests in the power of her body," which is quite sufficient for her to be happy, and she is wrapped cosily in the love of her relatives and friends. Lady Minne scorns her for the exclusive concern for her physical well-being; in the end, the soul is persuaded to search for her divine lover, whose welcoming behavior is described in explicitly sensual and physical images. This dialogue can be read as commentary on the vision described in book 2, chapter 3.[8]

Mechthild's attitude toward the body appears to consist of three conflicting dimensions: a secular acknowledgment and enjoyment of harmony between body and soul, a religiously inspired renunciation and devaluation of this harmony, and, finally, the reappearance and reconciliation of the two symbolic entities in visionary eschatological imagination. All three levels appear throughout *The Flowing Light of the Godhead:* the first one recognized but ultimately rejected, the second in battle with the third. It is as much a

8. The description of the meeting between the two is one of the few ecstatic instances in book 2. "He greets her with his lovely eyes, when the lovers truly see each other. He kissed her over and over again with his divine mouth—oh, blessings to you, blessings to you because of the very beautiful hour! He loves her with all his might on the bed of love. So she enters highest bliss, and in the sweetest pain she becomes truly aware of him." We do not know how Mechthild's secular environment reacted to these erotic images. Did they think it was funny? Witty? Pious? Extravagant? Werner (1976, 120) mentions a Frankfurt manuscript from the fifteenth century, according to which some Beguines prayed naked in their convents as their way of serving God. Werner interprets this behavior in the framework of a theory that associates nakedness and openness to sexuality as an anticipation of paradise. He quotes John Gerson (1363–1429) as a reliable witness for the movement of the popular Turlepins in France, who subscribed to these ideas [we are also reminded of the transformation of this motif into the witches' Sabbath later on].

sign of Mechthild's psychological largesse as it is a reflection of her cultural milieu that she allows and explores the influx of secular erotic sensibility in her religious writing. It might well have been exchanged for an infantile or masochistic cluster of fantasies. Her frank concession that a nonreligious life indeed has pleasures to offer that are difficult to give up certainly indicates a high degree of personal maturity. Because of her acceptance of sensuality as a medium for emotional and spiritual experiences, Mechthild's asceticism and secular feminine values can merge, if not be reconciled, on a religious plane.[9]

The Mass of John the Baptist. At first glance, the vision in book 2, chapter 4 does not seem to be a didactic vision at all. Most of the information is given to the reader in the form of symbolic action. The narrative abounds in gestures, symbolic colors, clothing, and actors of human and superhuman character. Mechthild provides us, as before, with a short prologue, which concisely explains the meaning of this elaborate vision. The vision itself seems to be intended as mere illustration of her argument: "Oh, dear Lord, how useful it is that a human being be of good intentions, even if she is unable to perform them. That is what our dear Lord showed a poor woman."

In terms of Benz's definition of a didactic vision (1969, 150–63), the relation between visual and verbal elements is reversed, but it is clear that the function of the visual elements is a "verbal" one. That they can easily be trans-

---

9. On the other hand, Mechthild is aware of the traps a secular life can hold for women. It is very interesting, however, that the only female population Mechthild gives admission to hell are noble women: "Of women I only saw in there [in hell] high princesses, who courted a number of sins similar to those of their princes" (3, 21). Compared to the long list of male sinners in hell, contemporary females must have been judged much more compassionately by Mechthild—or at least much more leniently.

lated into discursive speech and were understood as such is shown by the contemporary reaction to this vision (see below).

The visionary narrative evolves from Mechthild's inability, caused by physical weakness, to attend mass—a topos found in the texts of numerous other women mystics. In a "miraculous manner," God transfers her to a beautiful but empty church. She does not realize her move to the spiritual plane immediately and believes that she is late for the mass she originally desired to attend.

As she ponders her situation, the church fills with marvelously dressed saints, apostles, angels, martyrs, and blessed souls. After much confusion (caused by her medieval sense of social order) on which group to join, Mechthild is directed to a place next to the Virgin Mary. The service begins, with John the Baptist presiding at mass. In this celebration of the Eucharist, Mechthild receives not a wafer but a bleeding lamb, which, once swallowed, sucks at Mechthild's heart.

We are fortunate to have two documents that illustrate the context of the vision and disclose its relevance for Mechthild's immediate environment. In 1261 a synod in Magdeburg ordered, on pain of excommunication, that the Beguines of that city obey their parish priests (Grundmann 1961, 331). Magdeburg's clergy followed the example of other synods. The first synod ordering Beguines to stay with their parish priests had taken place in Mainz in 1233, and others followed there in 1244, 1261, and 1310 (this repetition seems to testify to the Beguines' stubbornness). The underlying problem was that the Beguines preferred to choose exclusively Dominicans as confessors and spiritual advisors, thereby evading control and supervision by the local clergy. Mechthild probably wrote her second book between 1250 and 1261, which places it squarely in the period of struggle between clergy and Beguines resulting in the synod.

The second relevant document comes from Mechthild herself (book 6, chapter 36), years after she presented this particular vision to the public. The text appears to be a defense against a group of people who criticized the vision because a lay person (John the Baptist) and not a priest presided at mass. The vision was interpreted as an attack against priests, who alone enjoy the authority to celebrate the Eucharist. As can be expected from a woman as eloquent as Mechthild, she fought with sharp weapons, calling her attackers pharisees whose hatred and mendacity would not be forgiven without punishment.

Mechthild defended her vision's point of view with two arguments. First, she refuted the idea that John the Baptist was a lay person. Because the saint was so close to Christ and played such a crucial role in his life, John was much more than any lay person could ever be. While still in his mother's womb he had been consecrated by the Holy Spirit (2, 4). "No pope or bishop or priest can speak God's word like John. . . . Was he therefore a layman?" she asks provocatively.

Her second argument gives us an insight into her theory of supernatural experiences. Mechthild distinguishes between information received with physical sensory organs and knowledge gained through the "senses of the soul." These two types of knowledge resemble each other as the light of a candle resembles the light emitted by the sun. Her enemies made the mistake of confusing the two dimensions and took literally what Mechthild (perhaps with some chutzpah) claimed to be spiritually true. If we assume that the tensions between Beguines and clergy were a smoldering issue in Magdeburg, we can expect that Mechthild was to some extent involved in it and tried to state her opinion on the controversy (safely clad in the intangible yet authoritative form of a vision). Comments on priests are found throughout the book (for example, 3, 8; 4, 9; 5, 14; 5, 15). With this background, her introductory statement (at first glance innocent)—that if a person is unable to attend mass, good intentions can be sufficient—must have provoked the clergy who tried to stabilize their authority. If a vision can substitute for a priestly office, who would not question the exclusivist claims of Magdeburg's clergy (Poor, 1994)?

The concrete church-political situation, however, does not exhaust the multilayered fabric of this vision. A second and more personal theme—a matter affecting other women mystics—is also woven into the imagery: Mechthild's physical weakness and frequent illnesses. The inability to participate in a church service is sublimated into a heavenly journey, which she is allowed because of her "good intentions." "Good intentions" stand for her willingness to court God unto death. They become allegorized as a purple cloak, a headband of gold, and a little golden coin she offers during mass. Her noble dress enables her to approach Mary, who stands in the choir in the company of saints, martyrs, angels, virgins, and bishops. "Well, my dear, take courage! She took it for a great thing that the common crow stood next to the dove," Mechthild comments to her soul. Despite strong emphasis on herself, her personal experiences were likely intended to be prescriptive. In book 3, where she scolds fellow Beguines for their lack of devotion in receiving the Eucharist in "blind routine," Mechthild invents a large group of allegorical figures who chastise her before she receives the Eucharist herself: "Truth reproached me / Fear admonished me / Shame scourged me / Compunction condemned me" (3, 15). In book 2, she interrupts the flow of the vision to display the same attitude. "Oh, I, unblessed slough, what has happened to me! I am not yet as blessed as I saw myself up there." The balance between reality and an imagined, desired, and desirable world is delicate—as delicate as the transitions between inner world and outer, between the "personal" and the "political."

The Chalice of Pain and the Chalice of Comfort. Of all the visions in book 2, the vision in chapter 7 is the shortest and simplest. It begins with an elaborate account of the situation that triggered the vision: Mechthild is desolate about her physical weakness, a weakness that she feels is the major obstacle in experiencing God's grace. The description of her unhappiness fills one-third of the short text. When her soul encourages her to trust in God's faithfulness, she is shown a "great light" (reminiscent of the "most shining light" appearing at the beginning of the vision in book 2, chapter 3); in this light God appears in stunning beauty and clarity. The core of the vision is as static as a painting: Christ holds a golden chalice in each hand, filled to the rim with "living" wine.

At this point Mechthild interpolates an explanation that the left cup contains red wine, symbolizing pain, and the right white wine, symbolizing comfort. The third and final section of the vision is verbal. Merging the language of the Beatitudes with Eucharistic symbolism, God explains the meaning of chalices and wine: "Blessed are [they] who drink this wine." The wine of comfort is nobler than the wine of pain, but most noble are those who do not shrink from drinking *both*.

As the previous visions, the vision of the chalices is didactic. The image represents the condensed message, which is then translated into speech by the Christ figure and Mechthild herself. Since, as Christ and Mechthild explain, both pain and joy emanate from a single source— God—the apparent antagonism of the two is reconciled. It is most commendable to have the courage to embody both (drinking from the chalices as the act that incorporates them most radically and completely without destroying/transforming the texture of that which is being made one's own).

The vision empowers Mechthild in an intriguing way. Unlike the advice of her soul to trust in God's faithfulness—much as parents tell a child that they will mend whatever has been broken and hurt, thereby rendering her passive and dependent—the vision encourages Mechthild to act, to choose, to take responsibility for her spiritual responses. It is her choice either to wait for comfort passively or to confront pain in the knowledge that it is part of a greater whole. God does not say, "You must drink from both chalices," nor is the message that the red wine—suffering—is the better of the two because it poses a greater challenge. As she does so often, Mechthild surprises the reader with her realism. Without challenging the significance of suffering, she argues that the chalice of comfort is ultimately preferable to the chalice of pain. The term *comfort*, as used in book 1, also describes ecstasies. Ecstasies are desirable, because they mark participation in the mystical courtship cycle. True to their sublime nature, they occur more often in the soul than in the body and are less accessible than pain.

This vision has been classified as *Symbol-Allegorese* ("symbol-allegorizing") (Kemper 1979, 96). Mechthild presupposed that the Christian symbolism of the chalice was known to her audience and creatively transformed it into an allegory. According to Kemper, her appropriation of a widely known symbol can be read theologically as a change from the idea of cosmic salvation to a more individual and tropological perspective (Kemper 1979, 101–8). But are the cosmic and the personal truly mutually exclusive principles? Can we ever fully grasp cosmic meaning without translating it on some level to our individual experiential dimension? It seems to me that a juxtaposition of cosmos and individuum overlooks the psychological thrust of Mechthild's visions. The tension between the chalices as Eucharistic symbol and Mechthild's allegorical appropriation of them lies elsewhere. The vision reads as a midrash on the *healing* function of confronting suffering as consciously and openly as possible, which is one of the reasons that the Christian symbol of the cross is so effective. Her vision uncovers a psychological depth dimension of the Eucharist but does not cancel out its cosmic meaning: it is cosmic *because* it reaches to the core of human experience.

Purgatory. The vision in book 2, chapter 8 introduces the theme of purgatory in *The Flowing Light of the Godhead*. Later on in her life, Mechthild's visionary range expands to include other nonecstatic religious topics such as the Last Judgment (7, 37), the Antichrist (4, 27; 6, 15), hell (3, 21; 7, 39), and creation (3, 9; 6, 31).

In the history of Christianity, purgatory was first mentioned in connection with the martyrdom of Perpetua (d. 202 C.E.). The belief in an otherworldly place of purgation and punishment is detailed further in the writings of Tertullian, Irenaeus, St. Augustine, and Gregory the Great. As Jacques Le Goff argues in his controversial book *The Birth of Purgatory* (1984), the revival and elaboration of the concept of this place between heaven and hell was part and parcel of complex cultural changes during the twelfth century. According to Le Goff, the transition from a binary pattern (heaven and hell) to a ternary pattern (heaven, hell, purgatory) happened also in society at large: the distribution of power between the powerful and the powerless (nobility and their dependents) became superseded by a ternary class distinction between "warriors," "worshippers" (the rising power of the church), and "workers" (the growing number of urban craftsmen and merchants, together with farmers and serfs). Reflecting a growing awareness of justice and the development of a judicial system, the idea of purgatory expressed the need for a subtler system of punishment for sins, which could address the proportionality of the sin committed. Because the twelfth century, according to Le Goff, was also marked by a greater enjoyment of life, the growing concern about purgatory also testified to the need to limit punishment and to develop a more agreeable vision of the afterlife. Purgatory became reimagined as a place of the elect, not the damned.

Although Le Goff offers a brief chapter on the Beguines, he does not explore the social implications of such changes for religious women. Beguines offered the service of prayers on behalf of the dead for those unable to pay for the religious rites a male monastery could offer for their deceased relatives. They responded to the demands of a new "market" and filled an important social niche. For Mechthild, these services take on a decidedly feminine character: "My other children are the poor souls who suffer in purgatory. I have to give them my heart's blood to drink. When I pray on their behalf and look at their manifold distress . . . I feel motherly pain" (5, 8). The vision in book 2, chapter 8 can be interpreted as a proof Mechthild gave of her capacities as soul-saver, but perhaps also as a testimony to the Beguines' pastoral function for medieval urbanites.[10]

Holy women's purgatorial services were not always met without suspicion however. Hadewijch, for example, was openly attacked for such usurpation, and the Beguine Rixenda, who reported of her success at freeing souls from purgatory, was questioned by the inquisition in Narbonne in 1288.[11]

Thematically, the vision in book 2, chapter 8 picks up the notion of *trost* (comfort) from the preceding vision of

10. For other texts in *The Flowing Light of the Godhead* which depict Mechthild as intercessor for the deceased, see, for example 3, 15; 3, 17; 3, 21; 3, 22; 4, 22; 4, 25; 5, 5; 5, 8.

11. Hadewijch seems to have accepted the criticism of her activities. In vision 5 she writes: "In one thing I did wrong in the past, to the living and the dead, whom I with desire would have freed from purgatory and from hell as my right. But for this be you blessed. . . . Your goodness (i.e., God's) was tolerant of my ignorance, and of my thoughtless desires. . . . For I did not then know your perfect justice" (Hadewijch, op.cit., 276). A reference to Rixenda is made by Le Goff (1984, 331).

the two chalices. The roles have changed dramatically, however: whereas Mechthild was earlier the passive receiver of the Eucharist (2, 4) and the recipient of God's teaching on the gifts of comfort and pain (2, 7), she now actively engages in the cosmic process of salvation. The vision is staged as a response to a prayer, in which Mechthild pleads for souls in purgatory. God proceeds to show her the "horrifying" place in all its suffering. Mechthild, seized by compassion, bargains with God to release as many souls as possible, after first trying unsuccessfully to embrace the whole place and carry it away. All of purgatory is too heavy a burden for her, but she succeeds in redeeming a thousand souls (in a very similar vision in book 3, chapter 15, she induces Christ to save seventy thousand). Since the souls are still "black, fiery, filthy, burning, bloody, and stinking," Mechthild cleanses them in a pool filled with her tears. The pool of tears (perhaps a variation of the folklore topos of the fountain of youth) anticipates the promise of the vision of the Last Judgment (2, 3), when God will renew all his creations and abolish aging.[12]

Intimately related to the theme of eternal youth are the symbolic roles of ugliness and beauty in the transformation of the sinners. Beauty, we have already seen, plays an important role in the transformation of bodies (2, 3). Later on in her book, Mechthild repeatedly uses the notion of beauty to describe the soul (for example, 5, 4: "The soul is as beautiful in her body as in heaven"), the elements of the relation of soul and God (3, 11: "When the loving soul looks into the eternal mirror, she speaks: 'O Lord, between you and me, all things are beautiful.'"); resurrected bodies, which "lie very beau-

12. For a late pictorial description see, for example, the central panel of a triptych by Jean Bellegambe of Douai, ca. 1520, with two allegories, Love and Hope, in Campbell, 1949, plate 17.

tifully above the ether and above the stars" (5, 9); and even earthly things and creatures, which "greet [Mechthild's] heart and lighten . . . [her] senses, and bind . . . [her] soul so deliciously" (6, 5). For Mechthild, beauty transforms, and through beautiful living beings we can perceive God: "In the nobility of creatures, in their beauty and usefulness, I will recognize God, and not myself" (6, 5).

In contrast to the beauty associated with salvation, it is the suffering souls' ugliness and repulsiveness that prevent their ascent to heaven: "Well, what should happen to these poor people? Because of this ugliness, they will never enter Your [God's] kingdom." Ugliness consists of the inverson of the traits of blessed souls, saints, or God. The sinners are fiery and burn just as Lady Minne is made of fire; they bleed like Christ's wounds, and, like Mechthild's earthly self, they are labeled "slough." Their dark color is in stark contrast to the light-drenched dress of the soul-bride (1, 44), and the dresses of the pious (2, 4). Souls in purgatory emit bad odor, whereas the blessed soul smells like ointment (1, 16) or is compared to a beautiful rose (1, 17).

It has been suggested that Mechthild's concepts of heaven and hell are based on the principle of an *analogia antithetica* (Tax 1979). Hell "is" heaven inverted; signs and symbols are reversed, but their structure remains. Hell is not a place of chaos. This inverted parallelism of heaven and hell seems to be true for heaven and purgatory, too. But here, the balance is far from static. Unlike hell's rigid order, purgatory's order can be broken up through human compassion to give way to redemptive beauty.

Sister Hiltegunt. The vision in book 2, chapter 20 is Mechthild's first to introduce another human being known by name into the spiritual world; the main actors in the preceding visions were of the spirit, not the flesh. The narrative thread unravels in a now familiar fashion:

the vision begins during prayer, and then heaven is opened. Interestingly, Mechthild cannot tell how she entered it—whether she was transported up or whether the divine place was lowered down to her. As is typical of a didactic vision, images serve only to set the stage for extensive speech, in this case a long dialogue between Mechthild and the late Hiltegunt. The central image, which initiates the dialogue, is a highly adorned Hiltegunt, who is posited motionless, it seems, before God: "Hiltegunt stood in front of the heavenly father's throne, adorned as a new bride whom the king has brought into his house. She was dressed in three coats and wore seven crowns on her head, and the nine choirs praised her in a special way."

What makes this vision so fascinating is that Mechthild has an opportunity to describe a woman of flesh and blood whom she knew, not merely an imaginative ideal such as Mary. Because Hiltegunt was known to others in her community, we may assume that Mechthild was also forced to be relatively realistic in her portrayal. Mechthild admired Hiltegunt and desired to learn from her as much as possible in the limited amount of time she had during a visionary state. She writes that her account communicates only a fraction of what her mentor told her.

The allegorical color and patterns of Hiltegunt's cloaks and crowns and the angelic music in praise of her denote a person of admirable religious fervor and strength. Hiltegunt is described as a zealous ascetic, compassionate, generous, chaste, strong, just, and wise. Her only flaw, the case for Mechthild's intercession ("Dear, where is the crown of humility, which suits spiritual people so well?"), highlights Hiltegunt's strength, at least in our eyes: she was too independent and self-reliant. Her answer to Mechthild's probing question is evasive, yet honest: "I did not really have it [humility] and earned just enough of it so that God could take away my arrogance." It is interesting that the lack of humility is also the one sin that blemishes another pious Beguine and confines her to purgatory after her death (5, 5). This nameless woman, whose asceticism was so extreme that "her nature withered away so much that she had to die," was acting exclusively upon her own judgment without accepting the counseling of others. As in the vision of Hiltegunt, Mechthild's response is gentle and compassionate; she even challenges God: "what pity it is that a human being experiences pain [in purgatory] because she accepted such sacred suffering [imposed by her asceticism] for the sake of her love [for God]." Her concern for the nameless Beguine is crowned with success. God lets compassion overrule justice: instead of seventeen years, the Beguine will only spend seventeen months in purgatory.

Both visions reveal a positive aspect in Mechthild's relationship to other women: she speaks up for another woman and defends her, and she can respect a woman as teacher and role model.

The ideal of a Beguine as represented by Hiltegunt stresses activity (good works, lavish compassion), strength, firmness (faithfulness, steadfastness), and intelligence ("holy" reason, truthfulness, wisdom). Her courtship of God is marked by "sweet desire," freely chosen poverty, and a *Minne* that is private ("hidden in my soul and senses," says Hiltegunt) and often painful.

The picture Mechthild draws of a woman she greatly admired and recommended as model for others can be read as complementary to the feminine images of Mary, Minne, and Lady Pain. All three reappear—somewhat modified and diluted, to be sure—in Hiltegunt's personality, at least as it was remembered by Mechthild: Mary's chastity and compassion; Minne's wisdom, strength, and independence; and Lady Pain's toughness (said Hiltegunt,

"I was a martyr of fiery Minne, so much so that my heart's blood poured over my head").

Perhaps because Hiltegunt's integrity and strength (much like the nameless Beguine's independence of will) are too threatening, and her ascetic fierceness too passionate in a patriarchal context, Mechthild softens Hiltegunt's image by a stunning contrast. Mechthild depicts herself as a lame dog, licking its wounds—a futile, misdirected pursuit—and overwhelmed by sorrow. The tension between a woman in all her strength and glory and a woman immobilized by her misery could not be more dramatically expressed than by these two portraits. But it is God who sends the vision of Hiltegunt in the midst of Mechthild's misery. The theological implication is profound: lame dog and crowned bride are not mutually exclusive paradigms but coexist as condensed representations of the two polarities of religious feminine self-envisioning available to the author.

The Mountain. The final vision in this cycle evolves around the archetypal religious image of a mountain (2, 21). In the history of religions, the sacred mountain is a symbol of the center, the meeting point of heaven, hell, and earth.[13] Mechthild's vision has been related to ancient astral conceptions, a view supported by her image of the "sun-mountain" in other chapters of the book. In the Christian tradition, the mountain represents the center of paradise (Apoc. 21:10, related to Isa. 8:18), and the place where God is faced. For Hildegard of Bingen (1098–1179), for example, a mountain symbolizes the dualism of good and evil on earth (*Scivias,* I, 3: 19).

Although the vision gives no indication that it was meant as such, Mechthild's text reads like a midrash on

13. Luers 1926, 138–139. Mircea Eliade, *The Sacred and the Profane,* discusses the importance of sacred symbols of the center (1959, 36–47).

Psalm 24: 3–4: "Who may go up the mountain of the Lord? And who may stand in his holy place? He who has clean hands and a pure heart, who has not set his mind on falsehood, and has not committed perjury."

Who may go up the mountain of the Lord? For Mechthild, this question translates into who can receive visions. The mountain is an allegory of the presence of God. It is of such intensity that human beings can tolerate a view of it for a brief time only, a claim that we already encountered in Mechthild's theory of ecstatic experience: "At the bottom, the mountain was as white as clouds are, and at the top, it was fiery and clear as the sun. Its beginning and its end I could not find, and within itself it gleamed like liquid gold in indescribable Minne" (2, 21).

Then, in a short dialogue between herself and God, Mechthild elaborates on what the psalm describes as "clean hands and a pure heart." Numerous moral prescriptions prepare the eye to see, none of which are mystical, but all of which are rules for life within a community: to give selflessly, to forgive joyfully, to answer hatred and cruelty with love, to be without guilt and debt, and to allow unconditional receptiveness toward the divine.

This is perhaps the only vision that demystifies the visionary process and renders it accessible to all "spiritual people." The recipe is stunningly simple and defies all of our twentieth-century theories on visionary imagination. In Mechthild's view, to act with responsibility and to embrace the community we are part of also frees our poetic and spiritual imagination. In our culture, moral duty and artistic creativity appear to be mutually exclusive; we seem to be afraid of our creative potential and, as a consequence, can conjure up only terrifying phantasies of violence. Not so for Mechthild.

6

Feeling with the Body of the Soul

Understanding Visionary Knowledge

$\mathcal{V}$isions are a common phenomenon in all societies; despite differences in their content, they cross historical and cultural boundaries (see Goodman 1987). This observation helps us to separate the dimensions of "body" and "soul" in an analysis of visionary texts. Although all visions, because they occur in so many different cultures and eras, share the same physiological pattern of arousal, the great diversity of visionary images and insights points to the crucial role of religious teachings in framing and interpreting visionary experience. As my brief survey of Mechthild's visions has shown, the visionary draws from a given pool of religious knowledge, then rearranges its elements or adds new imaginistic material in order to answer spiritually relevant questions within her community.

In the following section I examine several psychological theories dealing with the relationship between various types of visionary knowledge and psychophysiological states. Unlike humanistic psychologies, these approaches generally build upon traditional research methods and assumptions. Psychophysiology complements humanistic psychological theory because it pays attention to the physiological events undergirding visionary *and* ecstatic cognition. Yet, as with humanistic models, its implicit biases can highlight only select features of medieval mysticism.

State-Specific Sciences

The concept of "state-specific sciences" was Charles T. Tart's solution to the dilemma that only very limited aspects of altered states can be properly analyzed within the framework of traditional scientific assumptions and methodologies.[1] Tart's work had been geared toward the development of a theoretical basis for future research on holotropic states. His goal was to unite the benefits of scientific rigor with the recognition that certain noetic aspects of holotropic states are state-dependent, that is, accessible only if researchers themselves are in the particular state of consciousness they are investigating. Tart was also sensitive to the fact that only a redefinition of the human psyche as consciousness rather than a set of drives, instincts, and the like could yield an adequate theoretical framework to accommodate spiritual data. The shift in focus from "psyche" to "consciousness" as a technical analogue to the religious term "soul" is perhaps the most radical and important aspect of this struggle for a new conceptualization of psychophysiological research.

Tart subsequently developed a terminology that attempted to bridge the gap between religious and psychological languages. He defined holotropic states as "a qualitative alteration in the overall pattern of mental functioning, such that the experiencer feels his consciousness is radically different from the way it functions ordinarily" (1980, 201). Later on, Tart refined this definition

1. The term first appeared in Tart's article "States of Consciousness and State-Specific Sciences" in Ornstein 1968 (41–61); this essay was reprinted, with minor changes, in Walsh and Vaughan 1980 (200–213). The following page references are to the latter edition.

and stressed that the *patterns* of awareness, information processing, and other cognitive functions during "ordinary" states of consciousness (hylotropic states) are replaced by radically different patterns and not just "feelings" during holotropic states.[2]

Despite the acknowledged difficulty in objectively observing holotropic states, which for the main part are internal rather than external events, Tart suggested four methodological rules of traditional science that should inform state-specific research: (a) careful observation, (b) the public nature of observation, (c) logical theorizing, and (d) the testing of theory by observable consequences. His innovative contribution, however, is the suggestion that state-specific scientific explorations should be conducted by highly skilled experts who can enter a holotropic state and remain simultaneously in an ordinary state of consciousness. Ideally, they should also be part of a community of scientists who are equally trained to enter and observe holotropic states. Tart's model of participant observation resembles Deikman's notion of the "observing self," in which a type of awareness is fostered that can observe and analyze experiences independent of the subject's state of consciousness. Although such awareness can be cultivated during hylotropic states, the intensity of some holotropic states and the necessity for an interpretative framework for analyzing experiences during altered states makes such double consciousness extremely difficult to achieve. Furthermore, given the current legal prohibition against mind-altering drugs and a cultural lack of interest in holotropic states, Tart's suggestion presents an almost impossible hermeneutical demand.

Tart proposed a number of scientific fields from which

2. For Tart's definition of the differences between holotropic and hylotropic states, see Tart 1975b, 13 ff.)

state-specific sciences could derive their format and direction. His selection—comprising biology, physics, chemistry, and psychology—still shows a conspicuous bias toward the traditionally scientific that ignores ultimately necessary interdisciplinary connections with the humanities. Only vaguely delineated "fields" such as the "understanding of mystical states" and research on "drug-induced enhancement of cognitive processes" are mentioned as areas that could possibly offer complementary approaches for the analysis of the noetic content of holotropic states (1980, 207). As Mechthild's visions exemplify, a study of cultural superstructures and frameworks has to be central rather than marginal to the study of holotropic states. For Mechthild, the content of her visions and the meaning of her ecstasies were more important than a mere change in psychophysiological functioning as such.

Tart's venture into the development of more flexible methodologies has not been joined by many other scientifically oriented psychologists.[3] Perhaps because of the difficulties in translating mystical content into rational scientific jargon, most research psychologists interested in holotropic states continue to work exclusively within

3. See Collins 1991, for a discussion of those few "new paradigm" psychologies. Tart is outspoken in his critique of traditional scientific methods: "Many of the most important phenomena of altered states of consciousness have been observed poorly or not at all because of the physicalistic labeling of them as epiphenomena, so that they have been called 'subjective', 'ephemeral', 'unreliable', or 'unscientific'. Observations of internal processes are probably much more difficult to make than those of external physical processes, because of their inherently greater complexity" (Tart 1980, 204). Although this point deserves more space than granted in an endnote, women's reality has traditionally been treated in the same fashion with the same arguments. Both served the same function within patriarchy: by creating a negative Other, androcentric Sameness as a state of consciousness gained a rationale for its existence.

the framework of traditional science. This attitude comes as no surprise. As Kakar (1991) and others have pointed out, contemporary Western culture, in contrast to Eastern or indigenous cultures, espouses an unsophisticated and undeveloped view of altered states.[4] It is hard to refute the argument that in the course of its historical trajectory, Western society's emphasis on science destroyed already existing knowledge and the pursuit of knowledge about the realms of contemplation (Wilber 1980). In Tart's case, it is ironic that science can still be claimed as a tool to recreate what has been destroyed by its historical representatives. We must ask whether traditional science, even in its modified format as state-specific sciences, does not indeed continue to destroy such knowledge with an outmoded paradigm that has amply proven its destructiveness in regard to nonrational mental processes. Or can science, if it becomes critical enough of its own implicit ideological assumptions and willing to go beyond its limitations, turn around and reverse our centuries-old ignorance? In doing so, will it remain "science"? In order to answer these questions, we need a deepened interdisciplinary exchange between scientists like Tart and scholars of religion.

In the following pages, I explore these questions by examining some of the possibilities and difficulties of such interdisciplinary encounters.

4. Daniel Goleman, "Perspectives on Psychology, Reality, and the Study of Consciousness" in Walsh and Vaughan 1980, 29–35; an over-emphasis on work and a devaluation of leisure and play allows only a limited number of experiential dimensions. The dominance of "normal" waking consciousness with its emphasis on rationality and utilitarian subject-object relations with the almost complete exclusion of any other type of consciousness (except dream states, alcoholic intoxication, and certain forms of mental illness) conditions a society to react indifferently or even negatively to any other state of consciousness. See Hammond 1985.

Scientific Definitions of Holotropic States and Mysticism

From a strictly psychophysiological point of view, a holotropic state can be described as "any mental state, induced by various physiological, psychological, or pharmacological maneuvers or agents, which can be recognized subjectively by the individual himself (or by an objective observer of the individual) as representing a sufficient deviation in subjective experience or psychological functioning from certain general norms for that individual during alert, waking consciousness," to give the classic definition by Arnold M. Ludwig (1969). In his study Ludwig discussed several aspects of holotropic states, including triggers that can cause a holotropic state, factors that influence their external manifestations, and adaptive or maladaptive functions. A holotropic state can be induced either by a *reduction* of exteroceptive stimulation and/or motor activity via prolonged stimulus deprivation (a so-called hypoarousal as, for example, in "highway hypnosis") and through extreme boredom, sleep, and related phenomena, but also through experimental sensory deprivation. The opposite holds true as well. A holotropic state may be caused by a significant *increase* of exteroceptive stimulation and/or motor activity and/or emotion (hyperarousal). Examples of such triggers and/or the states they cause are brainwashing sessions, religious conversion and healing trance experiences during revivalistic meetings, fire-walker's trance, sexual trance, ecstatic trance, or any other *prolonged* state of increased alertness or highly intense mental activity. As Fischer (1978) has argued, Eastern religions historically have demonstrated a preference for states caused by hypoarousal, whereas Western mysticism has tended to cultivate states induced by hyperarousal.

According to Ludwig, different types of holotropic states may share characteristics such as alterations in thinking, a disturbed sense of time, a loss of control (the ability to manipulate one's environment in terms of self-preservation is usually connected with a "normal" state of consciousness), a change in emotional expression, perceptual "distortions," a change in the meaning or significance of perceived reality, a sense of the ineffable, and hypersuggestibility.

As was pointed out in chapter 1, the functions of holotropic states can be either adaptive or maladaptive. Adaptive expressions of holotropic states can serve healing purposes (as, for example, in shamanism), further the acquisition of new existential, psychological, or religious knowledge (either of a subconscious or a spiritual nature), or promote the regulation of tension in a social group. Among the maladaptive expressions of holotropic states, Ludwig listed personality dysfunctions such as traumatic neuroses, acute psychotic and panic reactions, and the ingestion of toxins.

Perhaps the greatest discovery of traditionally conceptualized scientific research of holotropic states has been the great variety of physiological and, to a lesser extent, perceptual changes that can occur during altered states of "consciousness." The body, so ambiguous a symbol to Mechthild, has been acknowledged as a reliable indicator of at least some shifts in patterns of consciousness. Clues of these changes were provided by physiological phenomena such as brainwaves, heartrate, eye movement, and body temperature. Although it became obvious that the mind is capable of controlling the autonomic nervous system (see, e.g., Ornstein 1968, chaps. 33, 34, 35), only recently have attempts been made to carefully investigate motivation and changes in perception and cognition; for example, a team of researchers used the Rorschach test to

analyze changes in perception and their relation to the
religious belief system of practitioners of a Burmese Buddhist teaching lineage (Brown and Engler 1984).

The question remains, however, whether a psychological model such as is implicit in the use of the
Rorschach test can avoid a reductionist interpretation
about a subject's spiritual insights. As noted above,
Charles Tart solved this problem by redefining not only
psychology but also religion. But like Naranjo or Deikman, he hesitated to follow religious practitioners in affirming the objective existence of a transcendent realm.
He perceived state-specific sciences to be a bridge between spiritual systems and science, because both share a
common ground: not different realms of reality, but different levels of consciousness. For him, "some aspects of
organized religion appear to resemble state-specific sciences. There are techniques that allow the believer to enter an altered state of consciousness which are proof of
his religious belief" (1980, 207).

As in state-specific sciences, the "esoteric training
systems of some religions" consist of "devoted specialists, complex techniques, repeated experiencing of altered states of consciousness to the advancement of a
certain type of knowledge" (Tart 1980, 207, 208). According to Tart, one major difference between religious "esoteric" systems and state-specific sciences exists not in the
use of different cognitive categories, but in the attitude
toward theorization.

Tart assumed that a scientist is expected to constantly
question and modify her inferences from data gained in
holotropic states, whereas the religious "specialist" is
more prone to be tied to her belief system and strives
toward continuous reaffirmation of these beliefs. In his
view, it is therefore necessary to isolate state-specific
technologies from dogmatic content in visionary experi-

ences, and to determine the exact relationship between technique and the process of gathering new data. A state-specific technology "is a body of knowledge about *how* to accomplish certain things, often coupled with a certain amount of innovation for accomplishing accepted purposes more efficiently. . . . the important thing in a science is to *understand*, . . . while the primary purpose of a technology is to *accomplish* already accepted goals" (1975b, 40).

The assumed inflexibility of religious systems appears to stem from Tart's observation of the often authoritarian dynamics of "cults and sects," which dominate the area of spiritually invoked altered states in contemporary society: "It was the hope of many that religions were simply a form of superstition that would be left behind in our 'rational' age. . . . The irrational, or, better yet, the arational, will not disappear from the human situation. . . . I have nothing against religious and mystical groups. Yet I suspect that the vast majority of them have developed compelling belief systems rather than state-specific sciences" (1980, 211–12).

A more thorough look at the history of mysticism relativizes Tart's view, but it is instructive to note how differently mysticism can be interpreted in order to fit the interests of a particular psychological researcher. Tart, like Maslow, approaches holotropic states from an anti-authoritarian position. At their core, holotropic states are interpreted as iconoclastic and a challenge to the "hylotropic" status quo. The lonely religious founder, the visionary self-actualizer, and the new breed of state-specific scientists (of which Carlos Castaneda is perhaps both prototype and enfant terrible) are rebels against the powers-that-be. In view of Mechthild of Magdeburg's work, their position is not without historical parallel. Mechthild commented amply and angrily about members

of the church establishment who harassed and persecuted her and members of her group because of her
mystical calling. Since the visionary mode appears to be
inherently a creative process geared toward solving problems of cognitive dissonance, its product, the visionary
message, can never simply be a reproduction of an ideological stance. Despite his appreciation of the creative
value of holotropic states, Tart insisted that historically,
the noetic features of mysticism usually deteriorated into
a function of an already established religious system.
What can be saved from "ideological pollution" (my
term), however, are the states in their "pure" scientific
availability; thus, one function of state-specific sciences is
to guard holotropic states against cultural indoctrination.
Tart conceptualized state-specific sciences as the continu-
ation of a lost tradition of esoteric "science," hidden
within religious systems, that was often abused for the
sake of devising spiritual practices less threatening to an
existing social order (Tart 1980, 216).

In light of Mechthild's teachings, the interpretation of
mysticism as state-specific technology or even as precursor of state-specific sciences is problematic. It assumes
that induction of altered states was the primary goal of all
mystics at all times. As we have seen, this was certainly
not true for Mechthild: if we can trust her testimony, only
mild states of deep concentration and inner peacefulness
(as, for example, during prayer) were created on purpose.
More intense holotropic states of consciousness were experienced as either acts of grace or unintended side-effects in
her journey toward the beatific vision. In all cases, a change
of consciousness was understood as a means to an end, a
step toward deeper communication and profound human
transformation within the dyadic relationship of "God" and
"soul" (See also Sheldrake 1992).

More importantly, perhaps, the term *technology* is
loaded with so many implicit secular meanings that its

transference to a religious meaning system tends to dis-
tort the character of religious experience. In terms of this
issue, Tart's claim that representatives of "esoteric" religious practices were applying scientific principles is problematic, too. To use *The Flowing Light of the Godhead* as a
case in point: it is astonishing to discover how little emphasis Mechthild put on a nonpoetic, abstract, logocentric description of her ecstatic experiences, although
she considered herself competent to teach the conditions
necessary to create the possibility of ecstasy. In regard to
her visions, the claim of mysticism as a systematic, scientific approach becomes even less appropriate, because their
occurrence was perceived to be fully beyond her control.

Finally, consideration needs to be given to the spectrum of the social functions of altered states; it is not accurate to state that mystics as a rule were tied to their
belief systems. As I noted in chapter 1, any new knowledge gained in a holotropic state is filtered through already existing explanatory systems; nonetheless, their
activation or destabilization depends upon the motivation
and context of the subject (see also Turner 1987; Lewis
1971). Mechthild intended her teachings as renewal and
critique of the Christianity of her times. An illustration
that visions can create, validate, or support a new interpretation of already existing religious teachings is Mechthild's vision of the Mass of St. John the Baptist (2, 4), in
which the centrality of the priest during the eucharistic
ritual was challenged, or in her reinterpretation of the eucharistic chalice (2, 7).

Finally, Tart's argument can well be turned against
the scientist. Her commitment to a number of basic "beliefs" in regard to what constitutes "scientific" methods
and assumptions about reality curtails the possibilities of
unbiased and critical data analysis and restricts the empirical scientist as much as authoritarian belief systems
may block a mystic (see Kuhn 1962).

Typologies of State-Dependent Knowledge

An attempt to reconcile the scientific demands of state-specific sciences without sacrificing the uniqueness of spiritual perception during holotropic states has been made by the prolific transpersonal philosopher Ken Wilber. Wilber acknowledged that the "single greatest issue today facing transpersonal psychology is its relation to empirical science" (1980). He proposed that all systems of knowledge share in a structure comprised of three "layers": an instrumental or injunctive component (Tart's state-specific "technologies"); an "illuminative wing," which catalogues transcendental insights; and a communal structure, which organizes the sharing of a particular body of information (1980, 219).

Knowledge itself is accumulated through three different processes. Using the Augustinian metaphors of the "eye of the mind," "eye of the body," and "eye of the soul," Wilber distinguished between three heuristic operations: a rational ("eye of the mind"), an empirical ("eye of the flesh"), and a spiritual type ("eye of the soul") (1980, 216–18).[5] Each of the three types can circumscribe only the knowledge accessible to its particular radius of "vision" or awareness and is therefore limited in its informational ("illuminative") value (1980, 217). A "category error" occurs when it is expected that all three types of knowledge and data-gathering can deliver any type of information (1980, 217).

To judge mysticism just as another state-specific *science* is what Wilber would call a category error: the spiritual is qualitatively different from the rational and cannot be accessed by scientific means. Nor is it useful to apply

5. As Jan Bremmer points out, the expression "eye of the soul" is found in Plato, where it denotes the mind (*nous*); the expression is also used in the Pahlavi-compendium *Denkart* as name for an ecstasy-evoking drink (Bremmer 1983, 40–41).

knowledge in the opposite direction. The mixture of empirical and theoretical knowledge gained through state-specific sciences is only in a limited way relevant to the body of mystical knowledge gained through contemplation: the only area where rational and spiritual heuristic systems can overlap is on the level of the "eye of the flesh." This dimension encompasses mystical descriptions and experiences of physiological phenomena as well as empirically documented physiological findings in the state-specific sciences. Although this aspect of holotropic states was relatively unimportant to Mechthild, it satisfies a contemporary need for concreteness in spiritual matters. Yet as it has become obvious, an interdisciplinary study of physiological factors is hampered by the way mystics and scientists collect and report physiological data. Tart's four scientific rules for conducting research may serve as case in point: in comparison to state-specific scientists, mystics may have been astute observers and well equipped to theorize logically, but their experiences have not always occurred in such a way that "the public nature of observation" and "the testing of theory by observable consequences" were guaranteed.

To return to Wilber: the spectrum of altered states cannot be charted in full as long as the dimension necessary for a deep understanding, the "eye of the soul," is given too little attention on the grounds that it is "unscientific." Only when state-specific scientists acknowledge the implications of seeing with the "eye of the soul" and incorporate these implications in their work—that is, correlate as much as possible different ways of understanding and observing the intricate dynamics of the spiritual dimension—can in-depth research on altered states begin in earnest. Because such research has to be conducted with a variety of scientific *and* nonscientific tools and assumptions, Tart's model needs to be modified. Researchers should not only be willing to enter holotropic states themselves but need also to let go as much as possible of the desired "double vision" of participant-observer in order to fully experience a holotropic event. As a consequence, this methodological syncretism must ultimately be flexible enough to tolerate the personally relevant (such as in a biographically motivated quest for meaning on the part of the researcher) as much as the objectively scientific. It should encompass the reflective stance as much as the experiential; it should draw from different disciplines in order to interconnect the political with the spiritual, and the artistic with the scientific. But this multidimensional heuristic structure, germinating in Tart's and Wilber's models of state-specific sciences, is still more a theoretical demand than a reality.

Seeing with the Eyes of the Soul:
Visionary Content and Religious Tradition

If it is problematic to "see" holotropic states exclusively with the "eyes of the mind," so is "seeing" only with the "eyes of the body." Although I reject Tart's all-too-negative evaluation of the impact of religious doctrine on mystical experience, the fact remains that already existing religious imagery and doctrine provide some of the language with which the mystic understands and manipulates often overdetermined or iconographically vague visionary data gained through psychophysiological changes. Influential theorists such as Steven Katz (1978) went so far as to state that mystics cannot in any way transcend their particular religious background and tradition.[6]

In his book *Mystical Experience and Religious Doctrine* (1982), Philip Almond developed a hermeneutical approach for the study of mysticism which attempts to de-

6. For a critique of Katz, see Pike 1992).

lineate more carefully the relation between mystical experience, its interpretation by the mystic subject, and religious tradition. In a comparison of mystical texts and a number of hermeneutical models developed by scholars such as Ninian Smart, R. C. Zaehner, W. T. Stace and others, Almond came to the conclusion that a religious experience is crucially, but not necessarily, dependent on a belief-system.

Almond distinguished between two fundamental types of mystical psychophysiological experience, contentless and content-filled, and a number of context-dependent interpretations (1982, 157–81). Content-filled experiences appear to happen more frequently than contentless experiences; equally important, the content is often and crucially context-dependent. He proposed that mystical states cannot be defined *a priori*, but are determined by the interpretations of mystical experiences provided by the mystic as part of the experience itself; he called these explanations "incorporated" interpretations. For Almond, then, there are as many mystical states as there are incorporated interpretations of mystical states (1982, 157).

Unlike Tart and Wilber, Almond thus followed the lead of the religious subjects in their respective contexts rather than attempting to superimpose categories not used by the subject herself; neither did he distinguish between noetic content and psychophysiological technology. Regarding the acquisition of new knowledge during visionary states, Almond suggested that if an interpretation does not harmonize with the mystic's theological, liturgical, social, and historical context, it is likely that the experience itself caused the new and independent interpretation (1982, 182).

Almond relied heavily on a terminology and system of interpretation developed by Peter Moore (1978). Pointing out that the immediate data for an analysis is not the visionary experience of mystics itself but their descriptions of it, Moore suggests four major combinations of experience and interpretation as a basis for analysis (Moore 1978, 108, 109).

1. *Retrospective interpretations* are formulated after the mystical experience is over and related to already existing religious doctrines. Julian of Norwich's second book is a good example of a creative retrospective interpretation.

2. *Reflexive interpretations* are spontaneously formulated either during the experience itself or immediately afterwards. Tart's notion of the participant observation fits into this category.

3. *Incorporated interpretations* are in some ways a subcategory of reflexive interpretations; they pertain to features of holotropic experiences that appear to have been triggered or conditioned by a mystic's prior beliefs, expectations, and intentions. They can be either more philosophically oriented (reflected interpretation) or mimetic and iconic (assimilated interpretation expressed in images or dynamics of action). Joanna Ziegler's observations about Beguine spirituality as expressed in devotional artifacts illustrate the category of incorporated interpretations (Ziegler 1993).

4. *Raw experience* refers to features of experience unaffected by the mystic's prior beliefs, expectations, or intentions; it can be integrated through retrospective or reflexive interpretations and shape in turn future incorporated interpretations. Raw experiences are the most creative and innovative; an Eastern example of this type of visionary event is the story of Gautama Buddha's enlightenment under the Bodhi tree (see Collins 1991).

Almond's and Moore's model of the relations between mystical experience and religious traditions significantly modifies both Tart's psychophysiological approach and Wilber's concepts of "seeing with the eyes of the body" and with the "eyes of the soul." However, Almond's and Moore's taxonomy is complemented by psychophysiological research of holotropic states, since physiological and psychological dynamics thus create a feedback loop. To cite an example: It is well-known that one of the striking characteristics of drug-induced holotropic states is the change in sensory perception.[7] These mechanisms form an unconscious system of interpretation or "belief-system" that operates in the interest of the organism. Psychedelic drugs induce a change of interpretative "sets" or at least destabilize the perceptive system of ordinary consciousness; as a consequence, sensory information is reorganized in different patterns. The experiencing subject then can choose whether to use retrospective, reflexive, or incorporated interpretations in assigning meaning to the new patterns—or to create altogether new interpretations. The same effect can be achieved by meditation practice, although the results tend to be produced more slowly.

The "world" each of us knows is thus a world created by selective perception in interaction with our environment. Reality and perception are therefore not necessarily identical (see, for example, Watzlawick 1984). What we "see" is a prediction rather than an accurate image of reality: that is, the perceived is usually subordinated to a particular function of the act of perceiving. In addition, the patterns of perception are habit-forming: we tend to prefer already formed patterns to new patterns that might disagree with earlier patterns. This understanding of the dynamics of perception, however, has been experimentally confirmed only for "normal" hylotropic states of consciousness and the impact of hallucinogens. Almond's and Moore's model proposes the same mechanism for mystical states; the mystical teachings of a

7. The literature on this subject is legion; a classic is Houston and Masters, 1966.

religious tradition form a road map for the mystic who experiences a destabilization of the patterns of perception and interpretation that are in use during hylotropic states. It then depends on the nature of the experience and the willingness of the mystic subject to follow, to alter, or to abandon the road map.

The following samples of accounts of medieval visionary experiences illustrate the creativity that is possible even when the perceptual/ideological framework of a mystic's religious tradition is retained. Note that in each vision, physiological, theological, and psychological elements are tightly interwoven. This close correlation between psyche, body, religious teachings, and culture underlines the selective nature of any of the contemporary models discussed above.

Holotropic Knowledge as a Duplication of Hylotropic Knowledge

A vison experienced by Birgitta of Sweden (1302–1373) is an illustration of the meditative technique to recreate sacred scenes and sacred time for the sake of spiritual growth. In this case, a common Christian iconographic pattern, the stages of Christ's suffering, is reexperienced during a vision; Moore called this process of religious appropriation "assimilated interpretation" (1978, 109). There are no explicit expressions of doctrine; the "scene" brims with intimate, minute details (Christ's loincloth, the flow of his blood, Birgitta's position in front of the cross).

> And upon command He got rid of His clothes, and a small linen cloth covered His private parts. He Himself bound it around, almost comforted. . . . With the first blow of the hammer I fell into a stupor from pain and grief; and when I returned to my senses I saw my son

transfixed. . . . Many streams of blood ran down His face from the sharp thorns and filled the hair and the eyes and the beard, so that almost nothing could be seen; and He Himself could not see me though I was standing close to the cross, unless He did press out the blood by squeezing together His eyelashes. (Birgitta of Sweden, *Revelations*, 4.70, trans. by Obrist in Wilson 1984, 240)

What makes the vision so intriguing is the collapse of the temporal continuum and the hyperrealistic precision of the visionary image. That which is often still allegorical or poetically diffuse in Mechthild's visions becomes as sharply outlined as a material object in bright sunlight. Birgitta's visionary outrageousness is her extreme realism, which suggests that state-dependent knowledge does not necessarily imply the collision of two symbolic systems or mutually exclusive "worlds."

Visionary Reimagining of the Self in Holotropic States

In a visionary account of Catherine of Genoa's soul, (1447–1510), a more thorough destabilization of religious and secular interpretative patterns during holotropic states is documented than in the case of St. Birgitta.

I see my soul alienated from all spiritual things that could give it solace and joy. It has no taste for the things of the intellect, will, or memory, and in no manner tends more to one thing than to another. Quite still and in a state of siege, the me within finds itself gradually stripped of all those things that in spiritual or bodily form gave it some comfort. (*Opus Catharinianum*, translated in Catherine of Genoa 1979, 85)

Although her text follows the traditional ascetical topoi of "desert" and the practice of *apatheia*, the biographical and social context of Catherine's life adds a fresh dimension of meaning. The mystic self of the *via negativa* relativizes the significance of ordinary values in a medieval woman's life—marriage and its duties, obedience to a husband, even the habitual comforts of religious life.

Marguerite Porète (d. 1320) forces the process of de-stabilizing ordinary conceptual patterns even further. In an audacious series of images, she reinvents traditional symbols to create a supernatural vision of herself:

> Love [speaks]: This book spoke the truth about this soul, when it is said that she has wings like the seraphim. With two wings she covers the face of Jesus Christ, our Lord. With two other wings she covers His feet. With two other wings the Soul flies, and dwells immobile and seated. (*Le Mirouer des simples ames anienties*, trans. by Bryant in Wilson 1984, 214, 215)

State-dependent Knowledge:
Feeling with the Body of the Soul

> Then she looks at him and speaks to him: "Lord, give me your blessing." Then He looks at her and pulls her towards Him and gives her a greeting, of which the body cannot speak. (Mechthild of Magdeburg, 1, 5)

> In this manner the blessed soul is so sweetly immersed in love and so violently attracted by desire that its heart rages and becomes fidgety within; its soul flows and languishes in love; its mind is madly lifted up with violent desire and all its senses draw it thither until it wishes to be in the fruition of Love. . . . Thus, moving spiritually beyond time, the soul ascends into eternity and above Love's gifts into Love's eternity which is without time; and it is carried beyond the human way of being into Love and beyond its own human nature in the desire to surpass it. (Beatrijs of

Nazareth, *Van seven manieren van heileger minnen*, Seventh Manner trans. mine)

Although these examples from *The Flowing Light of the Godhead* and *Van seven manieren van heileger minnen* are descriptions of ecstatic states, I include them here, since they demonstrate Tart's and Wilber's concept of state-dependent knowledge. Mechthild's and Beatrijs' texts are the opposite of Birgitta's vision: Birgitta fascinates through hyperrealism, Mechthild and Beatrijs attract through polysemous mysteriousness. For them, the Divine is barely communicable in ordinary language, yet it is, in part, still physical and emotional.

When confronted with a blazing "raw experience" of the "Divine Mother" that renders him almost speechless, the contemporary mystic Andrew Harvey realizes the tyranny of language. He notes in dismay, "all my life I had worked with words, wanted to use them, to master them; nearly everything I had learned had come to me through words" (1991, 35). From a mystic's perspective, all the models discussed in this and the preceding chapters are mere linguistic approximations, wooden scaffolds that hide the beauty of whatever they are built to protect, repair, uncover. Mechthild, Marguerite Porète, and Birgitta of Sweden might approve of a study such as mine, but if they do, they may with hesitation. I hope to have shown how humanistic and transpersonal psychologies make some sense of what we today call "holotropic states"— not only from the perspective of an academically trained agnostic but also from that of a medieval mystic. Yet in the end, this study raises more questions than it answers. What "really happens" during ecstasies and visions remains ever elusive. If we agree with Almond (1982, 221) that our investigations need to be guided by the incorporated interpretations of the mystic herself rather than by fixed predetermined categories that ultimately only confirm already existing theories about science, mysticism, the nature of intrapsychic processes, and the like, we can use humanistic and transpersonal models as building blocks for a dialogue with unexplored territories of our minds that have searched for expression long before Mechthild of Magdeburg found the courage to write *The Flowing Light of the Godhead*. She advised her audience to read her accounts nine times. This study is merely a foreword to her invitation.

Bibliography
Index

Bibliography

Aers, David. 1988. *Community, Gender, and Individual Identity: English Writing, 1360–1430.* London: Routledge.

Allen, Paula Gunn. 1986 *The Sacred Hoop: Recovering the Feminine in American Traditions.* Boston: Beacon.

Almond, Philip C. 1982. *Mystical Experience and Religious Doctrine.* New York: Mouton.

Ariès, Philippe. 1981. *The Hour of Our Death.* New York: Vintage.

Assagioli, Roberto. 1981. *Psychosynthesis.* New York: Penguin.

Atkinson, Clarissa. 1983. *Mystic and Pilgrim: The "Book" and the World of Margery Kempe.* Ithaca, N.Y.: Cornell Univ. Press.

Baeuml, Franz. 1980. "Variety and Consequences of Medieval Literacy and Illiteracy." *Speculum* 55, no. 2: 237–66.

Bakan, Paul. 1980. "Imagery, Raw and Cooked: A Hemispheric Recipe." In *Imagery: Its Many Dimensions and Applications,* edited by Joseph E. Shorr, Gail E. Sobel, Renee Robin, and Jack A. Connella, 55–65. New York: Plenum.

Baker, Derek, ed. 1978. *Medieval Women.* Oxford: Blackwell.

Beatrijs of Nazareth. 1991. *The Life of Beatrice of Nazareth.* Translated by Roger de Ganck. Kalamazoo, Mich.: Cistercian.

Beer, Frances. 1992. *Women and Mystical Experience in the Middle Ages.* Woodbridge, U.K.: Boydell.

Belenky, Mary Field, et al. 1986. *Women's Ways of Knowing: The Development of Self, Voice, and Mind.* New York: Basic Books.

Benz, Ernst. 1969. *Die Vision.* Stuttgart: Ernst Klett Verlag.

Birgitta of Sweden. 1984. *Revelationes.* Translated by Barbara Obrist. In *Medieval Women Writers,* edited by Katharina Wilson, 239–45. Athens: Univ. of Georgia Press.

———. 1990. *Birgitta of Sweden: Life and Selected Revelations.* Translated by Albert Ryle Kezel. New York: Paulist Press.

Bogin, Meg. 1976. *Women Troubadours*. New York: Paddington.

Boulton, Brenda. 1983. *The Medieval Reformation*. New York: Homes and Meier.

Bremmer, Jan. 1983. *The Early Greek Concept of the Soul*. Princeton, N.J.: Princeton Univ. Press.

Bridenthal, Renate, Claudia Koonz, and Susan Stuard, eds. 1987. *Becoming Visible: Women in European History*. Boston: Houghton Mifflin.

Brown, Daniel P., and Jack Engler. 1984. "A Rorschach Study of the Stages of Mindfulness in Meditation." In *Meditation: Classic and Contemporary Perspectives*, edited by Deane H. Shapiro, Jr., and Roger N. Walsh, 232–62. New York: Aldine.

Brown, Peter. 1975. "Society and the Supernatural: A Medieval Change." *Daedalus* 104, no. 2: 133–51.

Bucke, Richard. 1961. *Cosmic Consciousness*. Secaucus, N.J.: Citadel.

Büttner, Theodora, and Ernst Werner. 1959. *Circumcellionen und Adamiten: Zwei Formen mittelalterlicher Häresie*. Berlin: Akademie Verlag.

Buholzer, Sonja A. 1988. *Studien zur Gottes- und Seelenkonzeption im Werk der Mechthild von Magdeburg*. Frankfurt am Main: Peter Lang.

Bunke, Joachim. 1979. *Mäzene im Mittelalter*. Munich: C. H. Beck'sche Verlagsbuchhandlung.

Burton, Jeffrey Russell. 1984. *Lucifer: The Devil in the Middle Ages*. Ithaca, N.Y.: Cornell Univ. Press.

Bynum, Caroline Walker. 1982. *Jesus as Mother: Studies in Spirituality of the High Middle Ages*. Berkeley: Univ. of California Press.

———. 1987. *Holy Feast and Holy Fast*. Berkeley: Univ. of California Press.

———. 1989. "The Female Body and Religious Practice in the Later Middle Ages." In *Fragments for a History of the Human Body: Part One*, edited by Michel Feher, with Ramona Naddaff and Nadia Tazi, 181–239. New York: Urzone.

Campbell, Joseph. 1949. *The Hero With a Thousand Faces*. Princeton, N.J.: Princeton Univ. Press, Bollingen Series 17.

Capps, Donald. 1985. "Religion and Psychological Well-Being."

In *The Sacred in a Secular Age*, edited by Philip E. Hammond, 237–56. Berkeley: Univ. of California Press.

Carse, James P. 1980. *Death and Existence*. New York: Wiley.

Catherine of Genoa. 1979. *Catherine of Genoa: Purgation and Purgatory. The Spiritual Dialogue*. Translated by Serge Hughes. New York: Paulist Press.

Chenu, M.-D. 1968. *Nature, Man, and Society in the Twelfth Century*. Chicago: Univ. of Chicago Press.

Christ, Carol P., and Judith Plaskow, eds. 1980. *WomanSpirit Rising: A Feminist Reader on Religion*. San Francisco: Harper and Row.

Clark, Anne L. 1992. *Elisabeth of Schönau: A Twelfth-Century Visionary*. Philadelphia: Univ. of Pennsylvania Press.

Clark, Elizabeth, and Herbert Richardson, eds. 1977. *Women and Religion: A Feminist Sourcebook of Christian Thought*. New York: Harper and Row.

Clausberg, Karl. 1980. *Kosmische Visionen*. Cologne: DuMont Verlag.

Collins, James. 1947. *The Thomistic Philosophy of the Angels*. Washington, D.C.: Catholic Univ. of America Press.

Collins, John E. 1991. *Mysticism and New Paradigm Psychology*. Lanham, Md.: Rowman and Littlefield.

Coulange, Louis. 1930. *The Life of the Devil*. New York: Knopf.

Cox, Michael. 1983. *Mysticism*. Wellingborough, U.K.: Aquarian Press.

Czerwinski, Peter. 1993. *Gegenwärtigkeit. Simultane Räume und zyklische Zeiten. Formen von Regeneration und Genealogie im Mittelalter*. Munich: Wilhelm Fink Verlag.

Deikman, Arthur D. 1973a. "Bimodal Consciousness." In *The Nature of Human Consciousness*, edited by Charles T. Tart, 67–86. San Francisco: W. H. Freeman.

———. 1973b. "Deautomatization and the Mystic Experience." In *The Nature of Human Consciousness*, edited by Charles T. Tart, 216–34. San Francisco: W. H. Freeman.

———. 1973c. "Experimental Meditation." In *The Nature of Human Consciousness*, edited by Charles T. Tart, 203–14. San Francisco: W. H. Freeman.

———. 1982. *The Observing Self: Mysticism and Psychotherapy*. Boston: Beacon.

———. 1984. "The State-of-the-Art of Meditation." In *Meditation: Classic and Contemporary Perspectives,* edited by Deane Shapiro, Jr., and Roger N. Walsh. New York: Aldine.

Delumeau, Jean. 1978. *La Peur en Occident (XIV-XVIII siècles). Une cité assiégée.* Paris: Librarie Arthème Fayard.

———. 1983. *Le péché et la peur. La culpabilisation en Occident (XIII-XVIII siècles).* Paris: Librairie Arthème Fayard.

Denzinger, Heinrich. 1955. *Enchiridion Symbolorum.* Freiburg: Herder.

Dick, Ruth Anne Abraham. 1980. *Mechthild of Magdeburg's "Flowing Light of the Godhead": An Autobiographical Realization of Spiritual Poverty.* Ph.D. diss., Stanford University.

Dinzelbacher, Peter, ed. 1989a. *Mittelalterliche Visionsliteratur. Eine Anthologie.* Darmstadt: Wissenschaftliche Buchgessellschaft.

———. 1989b. *Wörterbuch der Mystik.* Stuttgart: Alfred Kroner.

Dinzelbacher, Peter, and Dieter R. Bauer, eds. 1985. *Frauenmystic im Mittelalter.* Stuttgart: Schwabenverlag.

Dronke, Peter. 1984. *Women Writers of the Middle Ages.* Cambridge: Cambridge Univ. Press.

Duerr, Hans Peter. 1978. *Traumzeit.* Frankfurt am Main: Syndikat.

Duffy, Eamon. 1992. *The Stripping of the Altars: Traditional Religion in England, c. 1400–1580.* New Haven: Yale Univ. Press.

Durant, Will, and Ariel Durant. 1981. *Kulturgeschichte der Menschheit.* Frankfurt am Main: Ullstein.

Eliade, Mircea. 1959a. *Cosmos and History: The Myth of Eternal Return.* New York: Harper and Row.

———. 1959b. *The Sacred and the Profane: The Nature of Religion.* New York: Harcourt Brace Jovanovich.

———. 1964. *Shamanism: Archaic Techniques of Ecstasy.* Translated by Willard R. Trask. Princeton, N.J.: Princeton Univ. Press.

Ellenberger, H. 1974. "Psychiatry from Ancient to Modern Times." In *The American Handbook of Psychiatry,* vol. 1, edited by S. Arieti. New York: Basic Books.

Eller, Cynthia. 1993. *Living in the Lap of the Goddess: The Feminist Spirituality Movement in America.* New York: Crossroad.

Erickson, Carolly. 1976. *The Medieval Vision: Essays in History and Perception*. New York: Oxford Univ. Press.

Fanon, Frantz. 1967. *Black Skin, White Masks*. New York: Grove.

Fehrle, Eugen. 1926. *Zauber und Segen*. Jena: Eugen Dieterichs.

Ferguson, James. 1954. *Signs and Symbols in Christian Art*. New York: Oxford Univ. Press.

Finke, Laurie. 1993. "Mystical Bodies and the Dialogics of Vision." In *Maps of Flesh and Light: The Religious Experience of Medieval Women Mystics*, edited by Ulrike Wiethaus, 28–45. Syracuse: Syracuse Univ. Press.

Finnegan, Mary Jeremy. 1991. *The Women of Helfta: Scholars and Mystics*. Athens: Univ. of Georgia Press.

Fischer, Roland. 1971. "A Cartography of the Ecstatic and Meditative States." *Science* 174, no. 4012: 897–905.

———. 1978. "Cartography of Conscious States: Integration of East and West." In *Expanding Dimensions of Consciousness*, edited by A. Arthur Sugarman and Ralph E. Tarter, 24–53. New York: Springer.

Fleischhack, Erich. 1968. *Fegefeuer*. Tübingen: Katzmann Verlag.

Franklin, James. 1978. *Mystical Transformations: The Imagery of Liquids in the Work of Mechthild von Magdeburg*. Cranbury, N.J.: Associated Universities Presses.

Fremantle, Ann. 1984. *The Age of Belief: The Medieval Philosophers*. New York: Meridian.

Fromm, Erich. 1950. *Psychoanalysis and Religion*. New York: Gollancz.

Frye, Northrop. 1981. *The Great Code: The Bible in Literature*. New York: Harcourt Brace Jovanovich.

Fuehrer, Mark L. 1986. "The Metaphysics of Light in the *De Dato Patris Luminus* of Nicholas of Cusa." *Stud: Internazionali di Filosofie* 18, no. 3: 17–32.

Gardiner, Eileen, ed. 1989. *Visions of Heaven and Hell Before Dante*. New York: Ithaca Press.

Geller, Leonard. 1983. "The Failure of the Self-Actualization Theory: A Critique of Carl Rogers and Abraham Maslow." *Journal of Humanistic Psychology* 22, no. 2: 56–74.

Gilson, Etienne. 1955. *History of Christian Philosophy in the Middle Ages*. New York: Random House.

Ginzburg, Carlo. 1985. *The Nightbattles: Witchcraft and Agrarian*

Cults in the Sixteenth and Seventeenth Centuries. New York: Penguin.

———. 1991. *Ecstasies: Deciphering the Witches' Sabbath.* Translated by Raymond Rosenthal. New York: Penguin.

Goleman, Daniel. 1980. "Perspectives on Psychology, Reality, and the Study of Consciousness." In "Beyond Ego: Transpersonal Dimensions in Psychology," edited by Roger N. Walsh and Frances Vaughan, 29–35. Los Angeles: J. P. Tarcher.

Gooday, Frances. 1974. "Mechthild von Magdeburg and Hadewijch of Antwerp: A Comparison." *Ons Geestelijk Erf* 48, 305–62.

Goodich, Michael. 1973. "Childhood and Adolescence Among the Thirteenth-Century Saints." *History of Childhood Quarterly* 1, no. 2: 285–309.

———. 1981. "The Contours of Female Piety in Later Medieval Hagiography." *Church History* 50: 20–32.

Goodman, Felicitas D. 1987. "Visions." In *The Encyclopedia of Religion,* vol. 15, edited by Mircea Eliade, 282–88. New York: Macmillan.

Gregory, Richard L. 1987. *The Oxford Companion to the Mind.* Oxford: Oxford Univ. Press.

Grof, Stanislav. 1985. *Beyond the Brain: Birth, Death, and Transcendence in Psychotherapy.* Albany: State Univ. of New York Press.

Grundmann, Herbert. 1936. "Die Frauen und die Literatur im Mittelalter." *Archiv für Kulturgeschichte* 26, no. 2: 129–61.

———. 1961. *Religiöse Bewegungen im Mittelalter.* Hildesheim: Georg Holms Verlagsbuchhandlung.

Guarnieri, Romana. 1965. *Il movimento del Libero Spirito. Testi e documenti. Archivio italiano per la storia della pieta* 4: 353–708.

Haas, Alois. 1975. "Die Struktur der mystischen Erfahrung nach Mechthild von Magdeburg." *Freiburger Zeitschrift für Philosophie und Theologie* 22: 3–34.

———. 1979. *Sermo Mysticus.* Freiburg, Switzerland: Universitätsverlag.

Harvey, Andrew. 1991. *Hidden Journey: A Spiritual Awakening.* New York: Holt.

Hammond, Phillip E. 1985. *The Sacred in a Secular Age: Toward Revision in the Scientific Study of Religion.* Berkeley: Univ. of California Press.

Happold, F. C. 1981. *Mysticism: A Study and an Anthology.* New York: Penguin.

Haug, Walter, ed. 1979. *Formen und Funktionen der Allegorie.* Stuttgart: J. B. Metzlersche Verlagbuchhandlung.

Hildegard of Bingen. 1990. *Scivias.* Translated by Columba Hart and Jane Bishop. New York: Paulist.

Hinz, Sigrid. *Das Magdeburger Stadtbild in 6 Jahrhunderten.* [Catalogue of the history museum in Magdeburg, 11/29/1959–3/20/1960.]

Holm, Nils G., ed. 1982. *Religious Ecstasy.* Stockholm: Almqvist and Wiksell.

Hooks, Bell. 1993. *Sisters of the Yam: Black Women and Self-Recovery.* Boston: South End Press.

Hopper, Vincent Foster. 1969. *Medieval Number Symbolism: Its Sources, Meaning, and Influence on Thought and Expression.* New York: Copper Square.

Houston, Jean, and R. E. L. Masters, eds. 1966. *The Varieties of Psychedelic Experience.* New York: Dell.

Houston, Walter Clark. 1969. *Chemical Ecstasy: Psychedelic Drugs and Religion.* New York: Sheed and Ward.

Hughes, Muriel Joy. 1943. *Women Healers in Medieval Life and Literature.* New York: King's Crown.

———. 1984. "Yonec." In *Medieval Women Writers,* ed. Katharina M. Wilson. Athens: Univ. of Georgia Press.

Hummel, Regine. 1989. *Mystische Modelle im 12.Jahrhundert: St. Trudperter Hoheslied, Bernhard von Clairvaux, Wilhelm von St. Thierry.* Göppingen: Kümmerle Verlag.

Idel, Moshe. 1988. *Kabbalah: New Perspectives.* New Haven: Yale Univ. Press.

Iglehart, Hallie Austen. 1983. *WomanSpirit: A Guide to Women's Wisdom.* San Francisco: Harper and Row.

Jaggar, Alison M. 1989. "Love and Knowledge: Emotion in Feminist Epistemology." In *Gender/Body/Knowledge: Feminist Reconstructions of Being and Knowing,* edited by Alison M. Jaggar and Susan R. Bordo, 145–72. New Brunswick, N.J.: Rutgers Univ. Press.

James, William. 1961. *Varieties of Religious Experience.* New York: Macmillan.

Kagan, Richard L. 1990. *Lucrecia's Dreams: Politics and Prophecy in Sixteenth Century Spain.* Berkeley: Univ. of California Press.

Kakar, Sudhir. 1991. *The Analyst and the Mystic: Psychoanalytic Reflections on Religion and Mysticism.* Chicago: Univ. of Chicago Press.

Katz, Steven T., ed. 1978. *Mysticism and Philosophical Analysis.* New York: Oxford Univ. Press.

———. 1983. *Mysticism and Religious Traditions.* New York: Oxford Univ. Press.

Kazarow, Patricia A. 1993. "Text and Context in Hildegard of Bingen's *Ordo Virtutum.*" In *Maps of Flesh and Light: The Religious Experience of Medieval Women Mystics,* edited by Ulrike Wiethaus 127–55. Syracuse: Syracuse Univ. Press.

Kemper, Hans-Georg. 1979. "Allegorische Allegorese. Zur Bildlichkeit und Struktur mystischer Literatur (Mechthild von Magdeburg und Angelus Silesius)." In *Formen und Funktionen der Allegorie,* edited by Walter Haug, 90–126. Stuttgart: Metzler.

Kieckhefer, Richard. 1979. *Repression of Heresy in Medieval Germany.* Philadelphia: Univ. of Pennsylvania Press.

———. 1984. *Unquiet Souls: Fourteenth Century Saints and Their Religious Milieu.* Chicago: Univ. of Chicago Press.

Kleinberg, Aviad M. 1992. *Prophets in Their Own Country: Living Saints and the Making of Sainthood in the Later Middle Ages.* Chicago: Univ. of Chicago Press.

Kluge, Friedrich. 1967. *Etymologisches Wörterbuch der deutschen Sprache.* Berlin: De Gruyter.

Kuhn, Thomas S. 1962. *The Structure of Scientific Revolutions.* Chicago: Univ. of Chicago Press.

Laski, Marghanita. 1961. *Ecstasy.* London: Cresset.

Le Goff, Jacques. 1984. *The Birth of Purgatory.* Translated by Arthur Goldhammer. Chicago: Univ. of Chicago Press.

Lerner, Gerda. 1986. *The Creation of Patriarchy.* New York: Oxford Univ. Press.

———. 1990. *The Creation of the Feminist Consciousness: From the Middle Ages to Eighteen-Seventy.* Oxford: Oxford Univ. Press.

Lerner, Robert. 1972. *The Heresy of the Free Spirit in the Later Middle Ages.* Berkeley: Univ. of California Press.

Lewis, I. M. 1971. *Ecstatic Religion: An Anthropological Study of Spirit Possession and Shamanism.* Middlesex, England: Penguin.

Lexer, Matthias. 1872. *Mittelhochdeutsches Handwörterbuch.* Leipzig: S. Hirzel.

Lightman, Alan. *Einstein's Dreams*. New York: Warner.

Llull, Roman. 1948. *Libre d'amie e d'amat*. Translated and edited by L. Klaiber. Olten: O. Walter.

Lochrie, Karma. 1991. "The Language of Transgression: Body, Flesh, and Word in Mystical Discourse." In *Speaking Two Languages: Traditional Disciplines and Contemporary Theory in Medieval Studies*, edited by Allen J. Frantzen, 115–41. Albany: State Univ. of New York Press.

Loomis, Laura Hibbard, and Roger Sherman Loomis, eds. 1957. *Medieval Romances*. New York: Modern Library.

Lubac, Henri de. 1950. *Catholicism*. London: Burns, Oates, and Washburn.

Ludwig, Arnold M. 1969. "Altered States of Consciousness." In *Altered States of Consciousness*, edited by Charles Tart, 11–24. New York: Anchor.

Luers, Grete. 1926. *Die Sprache der deutschen Mystik*. Munich: Ernst Reinhard.

Lurker, Manfred. 1979. *Wörtbuch der Symbolik*. Stuttgart: Alfred Kröner.

MacCulloch, J. A. 1932. *Medieval Faith and Fable*. Boston: Marshall Jones.

Mariechild, Diane. 1981. *Mother Wit: A Feminist Guide to Psychic Development*. Trumansburg, N.Y.: Crossing.

Maslow, Abraham. 1950. "Self-Actualizing People: A Study of Psychological Health." In *Personality Symposium: Symposium #1 on Values*. New York: Grune and Stratton.

———. 1968. *Toward a Psychology of Being*. 2d ed. New York: Van Nostrand.

———. 1971. *The Farther Reaches of Human Nature*. New York: Penguin.

———. 1983. *Religions, Values, and Peak-Experiences*. New York: Penguin.

Matter, E. Ann. 1990. *The Voice of My Beloved: The Song of Songs in Western Medieval Christianity*. Philadelphia: Univ. of Pennsylvania Press.

McDonnell, Ernest W. 1954. *The Beguines and Beghards in Medieval Culture with Special Emphasis on the Belgian Scene*. New Brunswick, N.J.: Rutgers Univ. Press.

McGinn, Bernard. 1991. *The Foundations of Mysticism: Origins to the Fifth Century*. New York: Crossroad.

McGinn, Bernard, John Meyendorff, and Jean Leclerq, eds. 1987. *Christian Spirituality*. New York: Crossroads.

Meadow, Mary Jo, and Ken Wilber. 1979. "Spiritual and Transpersonal Aspects of Altered States of Consciousness: A Symposium Report." *The Journal of Transpersonal Psychology* 11, no. 1: 59–74.

Mechthild of Magdeburg. 1956. *Das fliessende Licht der Gottheit*. Translated by Margot Schmidt. Einsiedeln: Benziger Verlag.

———. 1980. *Das fliessende Licht der Gottheit*. Edited by P. Gall Morell. 1869. Reprint. Darmstadt: Wissenschaftliche Buchgesellschaft Darmstadt.

———. 1991. *Das fliessende Licht der Gottheit*. Vol. 1. Edited by Hans Neumann. Munich: Artemis Verlag.

———. 1991. *Flowing Light of the Divinity*. Translated by Christiane Mesch Galvani. New York: Garland.

———. 1993. *Das fliessende Licht der Gottheit*. Vol. 2. Edited by Hans Neumann. Munich: Artemis Verlag.

Meissner, W. W. 1992. *Ignatius of Loyola: The Psychology of a Saint*. New Haven: Yale Univ. Press.

Meyer, Carl. 1884. *Der Aberglaube des Mittelalters*. Basel: Felix Schneider.

Miles, Margaret R. 1983. "Vision: The Eye of the Body and the Eye of the Mind in St. Augustine's *De trinitate* and *Confessions*." *Journal of Religion* 63, no. 2: 125–42.

———. 1985. *Image as Insight: Visual Understanding in Western Christianity and Secular Culture*. Boston: Beacon Press.

———. 1986. "The Virgin's One Bare Breast: Female Nudity and Religious Meaning in Tuscan Early Renaissance Culture." In *The Female Body in Western Culture*, edited by Susan Rubin Suleiman, 193–206. Cambridge: Harvard Unv. Press.

Milhaven, John Giles. 1993. *Hadewijch and Her Sisters: Other Ways of Loving and Knowing*. Albany: State Univ. of New York.

Monte, Christopher F. 1980. *Beneath the Mask: An Introduction to Theories of Personalities*. 2d ed. New York: Holt.

Moore, Peter. 1978. "Mystical Experience, Mystical Doctrine, Mystical Technique." In *Mysticism and Philosophical Analysis*, edited by Steven T. Katz, 101–32. New York: Oxford Univ. Press.

Morton, Nelle. 1985. *The Journey Is Home*. Boston: Beacon Press.

Muehlmann, Wilhelm. 1981. *Die Metamorphosen der Frau: Weiblicher Schamanismus und Dichtung*. Berlin: Dietrich Reimer Verlag.

Muschg, Walter. 1935. *Die Mystik in der Schweiz (1200–1500)*. Frauenfeld and Leipzig.

Naranjo, Claudio. 1973. "Present-Centeredness in Gestalt Therapy." In *The Nature of Human Consciousness*, 343–55. San Francisco: W. H. Freeman.

Naranjo, Claudio, and Robert E. Ornstein, eds. 1977. *On the Psychology of Meditation*. New York: Penguin.

Neumann, Hans. 1965. "Mechthild von Magdeburg und die mittelniederländische Frauenmystik." In *Medieval German Studies*, edited by A. T. Thomas and M. O'C. Walshe. London: Institute of Germanic Studies.

Newman, Barbara. 1987. *Sister of Wisdom: St. Hildegard's Theology of the Feminine*. Berkeley: Univ. of California Press.

Ohly, Friedrich. 1958. *Hoheliedstudien*. Wiesbaden: Franz Steiner Verlag.

Ornstein, Robert E., ed. 1968. *The Nature of Human Consciousness*. San Francisco: W. H. Freeman.

———. 1972. *The Psychology of Consciousness*. San Francisco: W. H. Freeman.

Pelikan, Jaroslav. 1978. *The Growth of Medieval Theology (600–1300)*. Chicago: Univ. of Chicago Press.

Perrone, Bobette, H. Henrietta Stockel, and Victoria Krueger. 1989. *Medicine Women, Curanderas, and Women Doctors*. Norman: Univ. of Oklahoma Press.

Perry, Ray C., ed. 1957. *Late Medieval Mysticism*. Philadelphia: Westminster.

Petroff, Elizabeth Alvilda, ed. 1979. *Consolation of the Blessed*. New York: Alta Gaia Society.

———. 1986. *Medieval Women's Visionary Literature*. New York: Oxford Univ. Press.

———. 1994. *Body and Soul: Essays on Medieval Women and Mysticism*. New York: Oxford Univ. Press.

Pfister, Oskar. 1904. "Hysterie und Mystik bei Margarete Ebner." *Zentralblatt für Psychoanalyse* 1, no. 1: 10–11.

Pike, Nelson. 1992. *Mystic Union: An Essay in the Phenomenology of Mysticism*. Ithaca, N.Y.: Cornell Univ. Press.

Poor, Sara. 1994. "Medieval Incarnation of Self: Subjectivity and Authority in the Writings of Mechthild von Magdeburg." Ph.D. diss., Duke Univ.

————. "Female Authority in Masculine Terms: Mechthild von Magdeburg's Conflicted Texts." Typescript.

Pope, Marvin. 1977. *Song of Songs*. New York: Doubleday.

Porète, Marguerite. 1993. *The Mirror of Simple Souls*. Translated by Ellen L. Babinsky. New York: Paulist Press.

Portmann, Marie-Louise. 1958. *Die Darstellung der Frau in der Geschichtsschreibung des früheren Mittelalters*. Basel and Stuttgart: Helbing and Lichtenhahn.

Pretzel, Urich. 1982. *Mittelhochdeutsche Bedeutungskunde*. Heidelberg: Carl Winter.

Raymond, Janice G. 1986. *A Passion for Friends: Toward a Philosophy of Female Affection*. Boston: Beacon.

Rehm, W. 1967. *Der Todesgedanke in der deutschen Dichtung*. 2d ed. Darmstadt: Wissenschaftliche Buchgesellschaft.

Riedlinger, Helmut. 1958. *Die Makellosigkeit der Kirche*. Münster: Aschendorff.

Ringler, Siegfried. 1980. *Viten und Offenbarungsliteratur in Frauenklöstern des Mittelalters, Quellen und Studien*. Munich: Münchener Texte und Untersuchurgen.

Roberts, Bernadette. 1985. *The Path to No-Self: Life at the Center*. Boston: Shambala.

Rosaldo, Michelle Zimbalist, and Louise Lamphere, eds. 1974. *Women, Culture, and Society*. Stanford: Stanford Univ. Press.

Rosenfeld, Helmut. 1968. *Der mittelalterliche Totentanz*. 2d ed. Cologne: Boehlau Verlag.

Rougemount, Denis de. 1957. *Love in the Western World*. New York: Doubleday Anchor.

Rubin, Miri. 1992. "The Eucharist and the Construction of Medieval Identities." In *Culture and History 1350–1600: Essays on English Communities, Identities, and Writing*, edited by David Aers, 43–65. Detroit: Wayne State Univ. Press.

Ruether, Rosemary Radford. 1983. *Sexism and God-Talk: Toward a Feminist Theology*. Boston: Beacon.

Ruh, Kurt. 1975. "'Le Miroir des simples âmes' der Marguerite

Porete." In *Verbum et Signum*, edited by Hans Fromm et al. 365–87. Munich: Wilhelm Fink Verlag.

———. 1977. "Beginenmystik." *Zeitschrift für deutsches Altertum und deutsche Literatur* 106: 265–77.

———. 1984. *Kleine Schriften*. Berlin: Walter de Gruyter.

Schmidt, Margot. 1985. "Elemente der Schau bei Mechthild von Magdeburg und Mechthild von Hackeborn. Zur Bedeutung der geistlichen Sinne." In *Frauenmystik im Mittelalter*, edited by Peter Dinzelbacher and Dieter R. Bauer, 123– 52. Ostfildern bei Stuttgart: Schwabenverlag.

———. 1986. "Das Ries als eines der Mystik-Zentren im Mittelalter." In *Rieser Kulturtage*, edited by Walter Barsig et al. 473–93. Nördlingen: Verlag F. Steinmeier Nördlingen.

———. 1987. "Minne du gewaltige kellerin: On the Nature of Minne in Mechthild of Magdeburg's *Fliessendes Licht der Gottheit*." *Benedictina* 4, no. 2: 100–26.

———, ed. 1987. *Grundfragen christlicher Mystik (Wissenschaftliche Studientagung "Theologica Mystica" im Weingarten vom 7–10 November 1985)*. Stuttgart-Bad Cannstatt: frommann-holzboog.

Scholz, Manfred Guenter. 1980. *Hören und Lesen. Studien zur primären Rezeption der Literatur im 12. and 13. Jahrhundert*. Wiesbaden: Franz Steiner Verlag.

Schweitzer, Franz-Josef. 1981. *Der Freiheitsbegriff der deutschen Mystik*. Frankfurt am Main: Peter D. Lang.

Schwietering, Julius. 1969. "Die Demutsformel mittelhochdeutscher Dichter." *Philologische Schriften*, edited by Julius Schwietering, 140–216. Munich: Wilhelm Fink Verlag.

Scribner, R. W. 1984. "Ritual and Popular Religion in Catholic Germany at the Time of the Reformation." *Journal of Ecclesiastical History* 35, no. 1: 47–77.

Seppaenen, Lauri. 1967. *Zur Liebesterminoloegie in mittelhochdeutschen geistlichen Texten*. Julkaisija: Tampereen Yliopisto, Tampere.

Shahar, Shulamith. 1983. *The Fourth Estate: A History of Women in the Middle Ages*. New York: Methuen.

Sheldrake, Philip. 1992. *Spirituality and History: Questions of Interpretation and Method*. New York: Crossroad.

Southern, R. W. 1970. *Western Society and the Church in the Middle Ages*. New York: Penguin.

Starhawk. 1982. *Dreaming the Dark: Magic, Sex, and Politics.* Boston: Beacon.

———. 1987. *Truth or Dare.* San Francisco: Harper and Row.

Stein, Siegfried. 1963. *Die Ungläubigen in der mittelhochdeutschen Literatur von 1050–1250.* Darmstadt: Wissenschaftliche Buchgesellschaft Darmstadt.

Stoevesandt, Hinrich. 1968. *Die letzten Dinge in der Theologie Bonaventuras.* Zurich: EVZ.

Sunden, Hjalmar. 1982. *Religionspsychologie.* Stuttgart: Calwer Verlag.

———. 1984. *Kleine Schriften.* Berlin: Walter de Gruyter.

Szarmach, Paul. 1984. *An Introduction to the Medieval Mystics of Europe.* Albany: State Univ. of New York Press.

Tart, Charles. 1969. *Altered States of Consciousness.* New York: Anchor.

———. 1980. "States of Consciousness and State-Specific Sciences." In *Beyond Ego,* edited by Robert N. Walsh and Frances Vaughan, 200–13. San Francisco: W. H. Freeman.

———, ed. 1975a. *States of Consciousness.* New York: Dutton.

———, ed. 1975b. *Transpersonal Psychologies.* New York: Harper and Row.

Taussig, Michael. 1987. *Shamanism, Colonialism, and the Wild Man: A Study in Terror and Healing.* Chicago: Univ. of Chicago Press.

Tax, Petrus W. 1979. "Die grosse Himmelsschau Mechthild von Magdeburg und ihre Höllenvision." *Zeitschrift für deutsches Altertum* 108, no. 2: 112–37.

Tillmann, Heinz. 1933. *Studien zum Dialog bei Mechthild von Magdeburg.* Marburg: F. W. Kalbfleisch.

Townes, Emilie M., ed. 1993. *A Troubling in My Soul: Womanist Perspectives on Evil and Suffering.* New York: Orbis.

Turner, Victor. 1987. *The Ritual Process: Structure and Anti-Structure.* 5th ed. Ithaca, N.Y.: Cornell Univ. Press.

Waddell, Helen. 1961. *The Wandering Scholars.* New York: Doubleday.

Wallace, Anthony. 1956. "Revitalization Movements." *American Anthropologist* 58:264–81.

Walsh, Roger N., and Frances Vaughan, eds. 1980. *Beyond Ego.* Los Angeles: J. P. Tarcher.

Warner, Marina. 1983. *Alone of All Her Sex: The Myth and Cult of the Virgin Mary*. New York: Vintage.

Watzlawick, Paul, ed. 1984. *The Invented Reality: How Do We Know What We Believe We Know?* New York: Norton.

Weber, Hermann J. 1973. *Die Auferstehung der Toten in den Haupttraktaten der Scholastik*. Freiburg: Herder.

Werner, K. 1976. *Der Entwicklungsgang der mittelalterlichen Psychologie*. Vienna: Karl Gerolds Sohn.

Wiercinski, Dorothea. 1964. *Minne. Herkunft Anwendungsschichten eines Wortes*. Cologne: Boehlau Verlag.

Wiethaus, Ulrike. 1991. "Sexuality, Gender, and the Body in Late Medieval Women's Spirituality." *Journal of Feminist Studies in Religion* 7, no. 1: 35–53.

———, ed. 1993. *Maps of Flesh and Light: The Religious Experience of Medieval Women Mystics*. Syracuse: Syracuse Univ. Press.

Wilber, Ken. 1980. "Eye to Eye: Science and Transpersonal Psychology." In *Beyond Ego: Transpersonal Dimensions*, edited by Roger N. Walsh and Frances Vaughan, 216–41. Los Angeles: J. P. Tarcher.

Wilson, Katharina, ed. 1984. *Medieval Women Writers*. Athens: Univ. of Georgia Press.

Wood, Charles T. 1981. "The Doctor's Dilemma: Sin, Salvation, and the Menstrual Cycle in Medieval Thought." *Speculum* 56, no. 2: 710–26.

Wrede, Gösta. 1974. *Unio Mystica. Probleme der Erfahrung bei Johannes Tauler*. Uppsala: Almqvist and Wiksell.

Ziegler, Joanna E. 1993. "Reality as Imitation. The Role of Religious Imagery among the Beguines of the Low Countries." In *Maps of Flesh and Light: The Religious Experience of Medieval Women Mystics*, edited by Ulrike Wiethaus, 112–27. Syracuse: Syracuse Univ. Press.

Zinter, Edith. 1931. *Zur mystischen Stilkunst Mechthilds von Magdeburg*. Leipzig: Robert Noske.

Zum Brunn, Emilie, and Georgette Epiney-Burgard. 1989. *Women Mystics in Medieval Europe*. Translated by Sheila Hughes. New York: Paragon House.

Index

DATE DUE

JE 11 '04			
MR 11 '05			
DE 1 2 '08			
		WITHDRAWN	